PRAISE FOR TAHMINA WATSON

"Tahmina Watson has produced an excellent book on the startup visa that should be read by policymakers, entrepreneurs and others attempting to navigate and improve America's often challenging legal immigration system."

— STUART ANDERSON, EXECUTIVE
DIRECTOR, NATIONAL FOUNDATION FOR
AMERICAN POLICY

"Tahmina is the foremost expert on the intersection of entrepreneurship and immigration. We need the Startup Visa program now more than ever for our economic competitiveness and national security. This book explains the "why" and "how" around this important policy."

— TROY VOSSELLER CO-FOUNDER,
GENER8TOR

"Tahmina Watson's years of experience as an immigration lawyer is evident throughout the pages of *The Startup Visa*. In this updated, second addition, Ms. Watson outlines why the Immigrant Entrepreneur Rule (IER), formerly known as the Startup Visa, could be a viable solution for immigrant entrepreneurs, often stymied by the current visa options available. Ms. Watson delves into the history of the IER, from its start in 2011, death under Trump and resurrection by the Biden administration. The book also highlights several brilliant entrepreneurs who had to shut down their businesses and leave the U.S. who could have remained in the country had the IER been an option. *The Startup Visa* is an excellent resource for anyone involved with immigrant entrepreneurship, from founders to investors; those who love to geek out on all aspects of immigration law will devour it."

— NINA ROBERTS, JOURNALIST, THE XENO
FILES PROJECT.

"Tahmina Watson's *The Startup Visa* makes a compelling case that immigrant entrepreneurs have made incredible contributions to the United States, but are held back by current immigration policy. *The Startup Visa* makes clear that entrepreneurial energy is being pushed away to the welcoming arms of other countries that have created a startup visa because those countries recognize the job growth that comes from new company formation. *The Startup Visa* is a must-read for policymakers interested in American entrepreneurship and those who have fought for a startup visa."

— JEFF FARRAH, GENERAL COUNSEL, NATIONAL VENTURE CAPITAL ASSOCIATION.

"Tahmina Watson has unbridled passion for waking up the United States to the reality that it needs to foster and encourage new entrepreneurs who are either outside the U.S. wanting to come to the U.S. or are here and want to stay. She has championed the "Startup" visa for over a decade and now makes the case that the time is now to adopt this type of visa into our immigration laws. At least 21 other countries have a similar visa for entrepreneurs. Tahmina makes the case that in order to compete with the rest of world for the best and brightest, we must provide an avenue for these people to become permanent members of our great county. As she so accurately states: The time is now."

— JOEL PAGET, IMMIGRATION ATTORNEY AND MEMBER, RYAN SWANSON & CLEVELAND, PLLC

"Tahmina Watson's passion and deep expertise in supporting immigrant entrepreneurs shines through clearly in this comprehensive yet accessible read of the latest edition of her Startup Visa book. Her focus on being solutions-oriented is of value to any policy maker, elected official, or advocate seeking an education on the landscape facing immigrant entrepreneurs and the broader setting of innovation-focused economic development for America. The key to innovation-based American job creation in the 21st century can be found in the pages within Tahmina's exceptional book."

— CRAIG MONTUORI, EXECUTIVE DIRECTOR, GLOBAL ENTREPRENEUR IN RESIDENCE (GLOBAL EIR)

"The Startup Visa is an important book on how the U.S. can continue to attract the entrepreneurial talent needed to lead the industries of the future. Tahmina provides valuable lessons on the history and current state of the U.S. immigration regulations and the issues they present."

— MATTHEW SAWYER, ADJ. PROFESSOR AT COLUMBIA UNIVERSITY AND MANAGING DIRECTOR AT ROCKET MARKET DEVELOPMENT LLC

THE STARTUP VISA

KEY TO JOB GROWTH AND ECONOMIC PROSPERITY
IN AMERICA – SECOND EDITION

TAHMINA WATSON

Edited by
LORNET TURNBULL

Published by Watson Immigration Law, Seattle, Washington, USA
www.watsonimmigrationlaw.com

Ebook ISBN: 978-1-7357585-4-1
Paperback ISBN: 978-1-7357585-3-4

Lornet Turnbull, Managing Editor

Caroline Doughty, Editor

Cover design by Raffy Ferras Hoylar

Author's photograph by Michael Doucett

Dedicated to my mother who had a vision for me from the day I was born, to my husband who helped make that vision become reality, and to my daughters who inspire me every day.

And, to all the immigrants - essential, hardworking, innovative and compassionate - who kept America functioning throughout the Covid-19 pandemic.

ACKNOWLEDGMENTS

There are many people who were instrumental in the creation of this labor of love, proving that it takes a village to conjure up a book.

While the law did not change since 2015 to bring us a Startup Visa, so much in the world has changed including a myriad of policy and regulatory changes especially during the Trump era. Therefore, it took a lot more work than I anticipated to update this book.

This book would not be possible were it not for my immensely loving, supportive and encouraging husband, Tom Watson. A patent attorney and partner at his own law firm Amin, Turocy and Watson LLP, Tom is a devoted husband to me, father to our two daughters, and a savior of all of my technology problems. (Yes, I have called him to solve the printer problem when it was, in fact, simply unplugged.)

A genius in his own right, Tom listens to all my passionate immigration arguments, even when I can tell it makes no sense to him. He prints pages of random, irrelevant statutes and bills for me at ungodly hours of the night, supports everything I do unconditionally, and even encourages this crazy passion I have to bring about change.

This book had its inception during a conversation with my client and friend, Mbwana Alliy, founder and managing partner of Savannah Fund, one of the first venture capital firms helping startups in Africa.

As someone who understands the intricate issues related to startups and the depth of my passion and legal knowledge for a Startup Visa, I will be forever grateful for his ideas and encouragement.

I must also thank my Startup Visa cohorts who constantly inspire, motivate and educate me. Craig Montuori, whom I have referred to as Magic Genie, has a wealth of knowledge and connections on anything about startups and related law and policy. Munly Leong, serial entrepreneur, whose unique entrepreneurial perspective brings an important element to the Startup Visa debate. Jason Wiens, policy director at the Ewing Marion Kauffman Foundation and former deputy legislative director to Sen. Jerry Moran, R-Kansas.

I want to thank Sen. Moran for consistently championing the Startup Act since 2010. His former legislative director, Mark Colwell, was a delight to work with during those early days. I have no doubt that Sen. Moran and his bipartisan supportive colleagues including Sen. Klobuchar and Rep. Lofgren will eventually be able to someday make the Startup Visa a reality.

I also want to thank some of my colleagues and friends who have been inspirational – Heather Redman, Managing Partner, Flying Fish Ventures, who is committed to finding a solution for startup founders. Thank you to Michael Schutzler, President of the Washington Technology Industry Association, who dedicated many hours working with me on the public comments for the International Entrepreneur Rule. Smeeta Hirani, my dear friend and a writer who helped me understand a little bit about the world of writing. Nicole Hay for being my first book reviewer. My colleagues at the American Immigration Lawyers Association, (AILA), who are constantly fighting for immigration reform and the rights of immigrants. Many of them are good friends, without whom I would find it hard to practice law.

President Obama and his administration deserve enormous credit for the executive actions of 2014 which lead to the International Entrepreneur Rule. The IER has gone through its own journey which I cover in chapter 6 in detail. I want to take a moment to acknowledge the Obama era White House staff members who worked on this issue including Tom Kalil, Doug Rand and Felicia Escobar. Their continued efforts lead to the IER becoming a reality in May 2021.

I thank my team at Watson Immigration Law, including Luka Jurić, Jacqui Starr, Bryton Tateishi, Cambria Judd Babbitt and especially Nicole Lockett. Without the team, I would not be able to spend the time I do arguing passionately for reform. They are my reviewers, editors, devil's advocates and fellow debaters on immigration policy matters that come up in the office.

Thanks to Jenn Morgan and her team at Radically Distinct, including Trudi Jo Davis, whose tremendous help made the first edition of this book come to life.

My profuse gratitude and thanks to my editor, Lornet Turnbull, without whom this book would simply not be complete–both the first and the second edition. She miraculously appeared just when I needed her most. As a former immigration reporter at *The Seattle Times*, she brings her immigration knowledge and journalism skills to help bring to life the vision and message I wanted to send in this book. I will be forever grateful.

For the second edition of this book, I am so grateful to Lornet, for continuing to be my editor. My heartfelt thanks also goes to Caroline Doughty who continues to help me publish my books after *Legal Heroes*, and Raffy Hoylar for the beautiful new book cover. Thank you to Cambria Judd Babbitt for her diligent research, help and work in putting together the accompanying Startup Visa podcast series for my podcast *"Tahmina Talks Immigration."* Thank you to Tamanna Jahan and Nicole Lockett for all their work on the startup visa series podcast audio and video work. I am so grateful to such an incredible team.

And finally, I want to thank my clients – all of them – for allowing me the privilege of helping with some of the most important issues of their lives. I want to specifically thank my entrepreneur clients who constantly teach me about dedication and passion, about the world of startups, and who inspire and motivate me every day to advocate for change so they can continue to change the world.

Thank you.

CONTENTS

FOREWORD – SECOND EDITION BY BRAD FELD

Like many Americans, my family immigrated to the United States from Europe and Russia in the early 1900's. As a profoundly proud American, I appreciate that I wouldn't be here if my great-grandparents and my maternal grandfather, who sought a safer and more secure life for their children, had not made that difficult journey. Many who try to immigrate to the United States today have the same story, goals, and desires.

I've seen firsthand many immigrants who want to fulfill their dreams in the United States but cannot because of our complex and archaic immigration system. Since co-founding Techstars in 2006, I have met many foreign-born entrepreneurs who have started innovative companies, contributed to the economy, and created good-paying jobs. I've also met many equally inspiring foreign-born people who could not do the same because of our out-of-date immigration system. I was motivated to learn about our immigration system and quickly realized that we needed a visa category specifically for entrepreneurs.

A fundamental belief of mine is that entrepreneurs should be able to start their companies wherever they want. The US's historical success as an entrepreneurial ecosystem has made it a place where entrepreneurs want to create a company, whether or not they were born here.

I was one of the thought leaders behind our first Startup Visa bill in 2009, which sought to create a new visa category for immigrant entrepreneurs creating new companies with their ideas backed by American investors. Even though nothing has come of that bill and subsequent Startup Visa bills, my belief in a Startup Visa's importance has increased, especially given the worldwide democratization of entrepreneurship.

In 2015, in response to Congress's lack of action, I co-founded the Global Entrepreneur In Residence (GEIR) Coalition with Jeff Bussgang, a venture capitalist, and Craig Montuori, a scientist, and philanthropist. GEIR helps immigrant entrepreneurs start their companies and seek assistance with their visa process. We launched in four states and later expanded to a dozen. In the past five years, the companies founded by these entrepreneurs employ almost 1,000 people and have raised over $500 million in venture capital. Imagine if we had this level of GEIR-related activity in all 50 states!

In this book, Tahmina Watson explains how a Startup Visa is a necessary component of immigration reform, especially as a global pandemic has brought significant segments of our economy to a standstill. Immigrant entrepreneurs help create solutions to the unprecedented challenges we face. We should welcome them to make that as a part of the U.S. economy, rather than blocking them and forcing them to do this somewhere else in the world.

I have followed Tahmina's work over the past decade as she was one of the few lawyers advocating with me for a Startup Visa. Though little has changed since our advocacy started more than a decade ago, her book is more relevant today and essential reading for anyone who cares about the economy, job creation, and entrepreneurship in America.

– Brad Feld
Managing Partner, Foundry Group
Co-founder, Techstars.
January 2021

FOREWORD - FIRST EDITION BY VIVEK WADHWA

The American Dream I knew is losing its luster. Restrictive U.S. immigration policies and the rise of economies of other countries are driving talent elsewhere.

When I immigrated here, America was the greatest land of opportunity for technology entrepreneurs. Standouts in science, engineering, technology and mathematics research flocked here, too. Now they can't get visas. Even as the American economy flounders, advances in technology are making an American reinvention possible. More than ever before, the United States needs immigrant entrepreneurs. These entrepreneurs, however, need America less than ever before. The trend has become so common that it has a name: the reverse brain drain. At almost every entrepreneurship event in Silicon Valley, I meet skilled immigrants on temporary visas who have great ideas, but can't start companies because of their visa restrictions. Visit Bangalore, Shanghai, São Paulo, or any other big city in India, China, or Brazil, and you will find hundreds of innovative startups founded by people trained in U.S. schools and companies.

Not surprisingly, the competition for talent has gotten more intense. Many countries, including Australia, Canada, Chile, China and Singapore, recognize the opportunity in attracting entrepreneurs, technologists, and other skilled workers. These countries are offering stipends, labor subsidies for employees, expedited visa processes, and other inducements to bring in startups. As a result of these aggressive recruitment policies, hundreds, if not thousands, of startup companies that might have launched in America, are now taking root elsewhere.

To attract that very talent back to the U.S., a Startup Visa is absolutely crucial. And it is the Startup Visa that first connected me to Tahmina. Her immigration law expertise, her first-hand experiences of the various legal obstacles, and her passion for the Startup Visa make her a clear leading authority on the topic and an exceptional advocate for change. No one has yet described the challenges of the current laws and policies as applied to startup founders with such depth and comprehensiveness. Her account of the ineffectiveness of current immigration laws reveals why talented entrepreneurs are actively choosing other countries to found their businesses and why action must be taken if America is to continue to lead the world in innovation. Tahmina's persuasive discussion is a must-read for anyone concerned with the economic future of America.

This book provides valuable policy advice and a guide for entrepreneurs hoping to navigate some of the treacherous waters of the American immigration system.

− Vivek Wadhwa
Author, Columnist,
Distinguished Fellow at Harvard University.
February 2015

PREFACE

It is January 2021 as I pick up this book to write my updated edition. I am still working on wrapping up my second book, *Legal Heroes,* which documents my work, and that of other courageous lawyers, during the Trump Era. But I feel compelled to raise this issue again – and with urgency. In the process, I'm learning how to work on multiple books at once, while juggling my day job of being an immigration lawyer, mother, and more. This is why:

As we navigate our way through the Covid-19 global pandemic that brought the world's economy to its knees, and as the new Biden-Harris administration begins the process of trying to bring this country back from the brink, we find a global landscape markedly different from even five years ago. Covid-19 has changed our way of life for good.

In 2020, about 50 million Americans were unemployed[1]. The housing crisis that began last year, continues, as people are being, or will be, evicted from their homes. (Some states still have a moratorium on evictions.) Our education system is barely keeping it together as remote schooling is now the norm and teachers, parents and students are all struggling to make it work. Many areas of America have inadequate internet. Our healthcare system is buckling under the weight of this health crisis.

The issues we face are endless and chronic. We need to find ways to pump new energy, new life, into this economy and get people working again.

How do we do that?

I don't have all the answers, but I have some.

As a lawyer practicing immigration law for almost two decades, I know that immigration can be a solution to economic recovery. An overhaul of our immigration system has been due for decades, debated for years and is now imperative. In this book, I talk about one aspect of immigration reform that promises to have a major impact on job creation, growth and economic prosperity - The Startup Visa.

You say: "Show me the money!"

I say: "Create the Startup Visa!"

My pursuit of this kind of visa started in 2009, the year I founded my firm, Watson Immigration Law. It was in the midst of the recession and I began to notice a troubling pattern: ambitious immigrants, eager to start their own businesses, were routinely stymied by a backlog in the system tasked with granting legal permanent residency – green cards – to foreign-born workers in the U.S. Waiting for these visas to become available left many of these workers stuck right where they were – chained to an employer and unable to break out on their own to pursue their innovative ideas. Our immigration system was failing them, falling short of its potential to retain promising immigrant entrepreneurs.

A similar situation emerged in 2020 when Covid-19 struck and a spotlight was on immigrants yet again. This time, however, they were part of the solution – part of the engine that has kept us going.

Remote schooling, an issue that still befuddles us, received a helping hand from a fellow Bangladeshi-American Salman Khan. His remote-learning model, *Khan Academy*, blazed a trail for many schools trying to figure out how to keep teaching even as they were thrust into unprecedented chaos.

The founders of Moderna[2] and Pfizer[3], companies created by immigrants, are literally saving lives with their Covid-19 vaccines. And the video conferencing platform, Zoom, is allowing us to function daily from schools, to offices, to election and socializing. Few people know that its founder, Eric Yu, was denied his visa eight times before he eventually was successful.

While there are many entrepreneurs outside the U.S. that could use the Startup Visa as a vehicle to create jobs and further economic growth here as these companies have done, there are tens of thousands already in the U.S., eager for the opportunity to do so.

The first standalone Startup Visa Act, intended to break that frustrating logjam and create a pathway for entrepreneurs, was introduced in 2010. The bipartisan measure was recognition by some in Congress of the critical need for a specialty visa that would help retain foreign talent, create jobs and grow the U.S. economy. It never passed. And each year, the need for it grows more urgent. My passion for a breakthrough is matched only by my increasing frustration as I've watched Congress, year after year, fail to pass legislation to address this problem.

This book is an outgrowth of a blog I began writing in 2008, along with other articles on immigration. It draws on my experiences as an immigrant, a lawyer and an entrepreneur – and those of my clients –

to help demonstrate and offer perspective on why the need for this visa is so critical now.

My hope is that it will influence lawmakers and policy makers, and especially the Biden-Harris administration, to strike now, while we have momentum and desire for change. And I hope that it will inspire a more informed startup community, including entrepreneurs, investors and everyone else in the ecosystem, to become better advocates for change.

INTRODUCTION

Change through technology has a powerful impact. Technology has revolutionized the way we work, plan travel, buy houses, study, conduct research, explore the world, cook and clean, buy consumer goods, get our news, watch television, communicate in real time from one end of the globe to another, listen to music and even buy our groceries. And technology has been a crucial part of our lives during the Covid-19 global pandemic.

We have wearable technology, which only promises to become more sophisticated with time. You can now print complicated medical devices – even houses – on a 3D printer. Vivek Wadhwa, an academic and entrepreneur,[1] and author of the book, *The Immigrant Exodus - Why America is Losing the Global Race to Capture Entrepreneurial Talent*, recently discussed how our current technological advances are catching up to all that we saw and marveled at in *Star Trek*.[2] By the next generation, travel agents, CDs and even the U.S. Postal Service may have joined the Pony Express in the closet of services that technology has made obsolete.

All of these changes, and so many yet to come, are possible because of the ingenuity and creativity of the people behind them – people from every corner of the globe who lead the world in innovation and technological advancements. But in order for innovators and entrepreneurs from abroad to apply that talent in the U.S., we must first provide a straightforward, workable and legal way for them to come here and stay.

Such a path doesn't yet fully exist – but it can. The Startup Visa would be one such path. It targets bright minds filled with cutting-edge ideas – those who have figured out how to apply lean business practices and use investor cash to grow their businesses from startup to success. Since it was first introduced in Congress in 2010, the bipartisan Startup Visa Act has had several incarnations. And despite broad consensus on its potential benefits to the U.S. economy, the measure has been hobbled repeatedly by political gridlock and has failed to advance. Subsequent measures in Congress to plug this gaping hole in the immigration system have also suffered a similar fate, leaving the U.S. without the necessary tools to attract and retain some of the world's best and brightest entrepreneurs.

With Congress failing to act, President Obama announced in November 2014, that he would use his executive powers to address immigration shortcomings where he could. And he did. The result was the *International Entrepreneur Rule (IER)*, which was set to go into effect in June 2017. However, upon taking office, Donald Trump all but dismantled this hard-fought provision that would have been the closest we've ever come to a Startup Visa.

This demonstrates why it's imperative that we have Congressional action to ensure a permanent solution to attract and retain business talent from abroad that is not bound by the mercy of a single administration. A Startup Visa, invaluable to high-tech Silicon Valley firms as well as other industries, will help create new businesses, generate new jobs and raise revenue for local and national economies. The Ewing Marion Kauffman Foundation, a Kansas City-based non-profit dedicated to advancing educational achievement and entrepreneurial success, states in its 2017 Kauffman Index, that immigrants are more than twice as likely as native-born Americans to become entrepreneurs.[3] Between 1977 and 2005, all net jobs created in the U.S. were by startup firms.[4] They generated 3 million jobs annually between 1992 and 2005.[5] A 2018 study by the National Foundation for American Policy, found that privately held billion-dollar startup companies founded by immigrants have created an average of more than 1,200 jobs per company.[6]

The Kauffman Foundation predicts that without a Startup Visa, the U.S. will miss the opportunity to create 1.6 million jobs over the next 10 years.[7]

How so? Other countries, Chile, Brazil, Italy, Canada, U.K. and many others, have recognized what the U.S. has failed to: that immigration has to be part of their nations' economic growth strategy. Not surprisingly, many of these countries are already reaping the benefits of their investments in startup firms.

Each year, the U.S. loses millions of dollars in revenue and sends hundreds of thousands of jobs to countries willing to embrace foreign entrepreneurs – many of them educated and trained at American colleges and universities, sometimes even at U.S. taxpayer expense.

Take for example the case of Kunal Bahl. Bahl, born in India, is a graduate of the Wharton School of Business at the University of Pennsylvania, but was compelled to leave the U.S. because of his immigration status.

In 2010, he founded New Delhi, India-based Snapdeal – dubbed the Amazon of India – which boasts more than 20 million users and employs more than 2,000 people in that country. In 2018-2019,

Snapdeal grossed over \$100 million in revenue.[8] Consider the job-creation and revenue generation that India is already seeing from this company.

In this high-stakes global race to attract and retain the best, the U.S. is rapidly losing its edge. Other countries embrace the immigrant entrepreneurs we turn away. Yet we remain the world's most desired location for launching a business – boasting diversity, top schools, enthusiastic investors, a nurturing business climate and a relatively stable political system. America is indeed the 'Holy Grail' for startups.

But we need to capitalize on those strengths. One key to economic prosperity is creating an environment that allows businesses and citizens to thrive. It follows then, that one solution to economic stagnation is not making it harder for foreign entrepreneurs to bring their skills and expertise to the U.S., but rather to welcome and nurture them on our soil – not blindly, but strategically – ultimately reaping the job growth and economic development benefits they will invariably bring.

The way companies bring forth forward-thinking technologies has also evolved. Because technology has become so accessible, entrepreneurs with innovative and workable ideas can start a company from anywhere – their basements, their garages or even their dorm rooms. But as the fledgling company begins to scale up, the need for money also grows.

Often, these companies rely on funding from investors – from seed funding to series A, B, C and beyond. Those behind the money, such as venture capitalists or angel investors, also play a vital role in bringing high-growth companies to fruition. They, too, see the benefit of attracting entrepreneurial talent from abroad. Indeed the National Venture Capital Association (NVCA), a long standing advocate for a startup visa, in a report showed that one-third of all venture-backed

IPOs between 2006 and 2012 were companies that were founded or co-founded by immigrants.[9] According to a 2018 study by the National Foundation for American Policy, "Immigrants have started more than half (55%) of all startup companies in the U.S., valued at $1 billion or more and are key members of management or product development teams in more than 80% of these companies." And nearly one-quarter of these billion-dollar companies had a founder who came to America as an international student.[10]

As an immigration attorney who works with many of these entrepreneurs, I find our current policies outdated and inefficient at moving people through the legal process. It ends up costing the individual, employers and the government unnecessary time and resources – and ultimately costing the country. Laws help us shape our future. And if we want a future of innovation and prosperity, then we need laws to enable it. Immigrant entrepreneurs bring a fresh perspective to business operations by virtue of their diverse experience and a powerful drive to succeed. The Startup Visa will help America recover an economy devastated by this global pandemic and help us regain our hard-won reputation as an economic powerhouse -- a leader among nations. Without it, we risk squandering a great opportunity and resource.

IMMIGRATION AND INNOVATION THROUGH HISTORY

Amerca is a land of immigrants. Immigrants shaped and fed its democracy, explored its interior, built its infrastructure and honed it, brick by brick and invention by invention, into the world's greatest economy. These immigrants came to this country from everywhere around the globe for its promise of freedom and unlimited potential. They came to build a better life for themselves and their children.

History demonstrates that, despite restrictions placed on immigration since the latter half of the 19th century, economic prosperity and increased immigration go hand in hand. In 1609, Englishman John Rolfe sailed from England to Jamestown, VA., a poor scavenging settlement, where economic desperation had created a cannibalistic colony. Rolfe was the first to figure out how to commercially cultivate a sweet variety of tobacco which became the start of a booming export industry. Jamestown and neighboring towns began to blossom almost overnight.

The industrial revolution of the 19th century is laced with many such stories, as immigrants continued to make a lasting impression on this still-young nation. And nowhere was the industrial growth more apparent than in New York City, where Scottish-born Andrew Carnegie left his mark. Carnegie came to America with his parents in 1848. The family was dirt poor. An inventor at heart, Carnegie discovered a process for mass producing cheaper steel, which helped transform New York into a vertical city. The city's physical growth brought more businesses and jobs and thus economic prosperity – the foundation of today's modern day New York City.

The story of how Procter & Gamble was founded is particularly captivating. William Procter was an Englishman and candle maker in Cincinnati and James Gamble was an Irishman who was an apprentice soap maker. The two men married sisters Olivia and Elizabeth Norris. Their father-in-law advised them to become business partners and like good sons-in-law, eager to please, they followed his advice. Thus Procter & Gamble was founded in 1837.[1] Today, the Cincinnati-based household products company has 99,000 employees worldwide.[2]

Yet, despite the obvious contributions immigrants have brought this country over the generations, it has made it increasingly difficult for them to settle here. After gaining independence from Britain in 1776, the U.S. Congress declared that any free white person of good moral standing could apply for citizenship after two years' residency. This policy remained intact for nearly a century. But slowly, laws were introduced to restrict immigration, generally on ethnic, moral or health grounds.

By the early 19th Century, America's expansion westward revealed the need for railroads, construction of which was severely hampered by a shortage of workers. Laws were created to allow the immigration of Chinese workers to address the labor shortfall. By 1868, some 4,000 workers – two-thirds of them Chinese – had built the transcontinental railroad.[3] Without them, we would not have the railroad infrastructure that today allows the free movement of goods and services across the United States. During this period, some famous retailers were established, one of whom would go on to create what is today a world-famous brand. Levi Strauss, born in Germany in 1829, emigrated with his mother and two sisters to the U.S. in 1847. They joined his two brothers in New York, where young Strauss worked in their dry goods business. After becoming a U.S. citizen in 1853, he moved to San Francisco, during the height of the Gold Rush.[4]

He opened a small dry-goods business as his brothers' West Coast agent and there he sold a successful line of fabrics and clothing. His brother-in-law, David Stern, a tailor from Nevada, told Strauss how he could use metal rivets in certain areas of stress on a pair of pants to prevent tear. At that time, miners and other laborers complained their clothes weren't durable enough. Strauss paid for a patent under Levi Strauss & Co., and in 1873 the blue jeans brand was born. A century and a half later, Levi Strauss' jeans are just as popular and fashionable. More importantly, the global company's contribution to the U.S. economy is unquestioned. In 2020, Levi Strauss & Co., reported revenue of $4.45 billion, with 14,800[5] employees and almost a thousand company-operated stores worldwide.[6]

As the country grew and expanded, nativism gradually crept in – primarily targeting non-Europeans. Just over two decades after creating laws to allow Chinese immigration, the Chinese Exclusion Act of 1882 was enacted, suspending Chinese immigration for 10 years and barring Chinese in the U.S. from obtaining citizenship.

And three years later, the law that had permitted the recruitment of unskilled labor was rescinded. By 1917, all Asian immigrants would be barred from the country.[7] This was followed by restrictions, primarily in the form of quotas and literacy tests, designed to reduce immigration.

In the 1920s, in the wake of World War I, piecemeal legislation began to gradually open up immigration, but in smaller, controlled numbers.[8] The strictest controls were placed on people coming from countries such as China, the Philippines and India. Later, those restrictions were formalized through the Immigration Act of 1924, which limited immigrants to 2 percent of each nationality present in the U.S. in the 1890 U.S. Census. It excluded immigrants from Asia entirely.

During the mid- to late 1920s, commerce, industrialization and transportation resulted in bigger, sprawling cities where many immigrants had settled. Immigration laws did not see significant changes during this time. However, the Great Depression of 1930, followed by WWII and then the Cold War, put pressure on the economy and society and there was soon consensus that an immigration overhaul was needed.

In 1952, multiple laws that controlled immigration and naturalization in this country at the time, were folded into a single, comprehensive statute which serves as the foundation of today's immigration laws. The Immigration and Nationality Act of 1952 did much to change the immigration landscape, including abolishing the "free white persons" of "good moral character" restrictions.

But more importantly, and for purposes of this discussion, it established a class of immigrants with special, technical skills, who were exempt from any quotas.[9] More than a decade later, Congress passed the Immigration and Nationality Act of 1965, abolishing the national quota system and replacing it with a preference system that focused on immigrant skills and family relationships. It also established a per-country limit, which still exists today.

The 1950s and 1960s gave birth to many renowned companies that today continue to make significant contributions to the U.S. economy.

They include retail giants such as Big Lots founded in 1967 by Shol Shenk, a Russian immigrant.

And who hasn't heard of Bose? It is perhaps one of the most recognizable brands of speaker systems. Dr. Amar Bose, a child of immigrant parents, an electrical engineer and graduate of Massachusetts Institute of Technology, was its creator. He was inspired to develop the high-end audio system after being disappointed with a stereo system he had purchased. Founded in 1964, Bose is today listed by Forbes as the nation's 167th largest private company with more than 10,000 employees and $2.67 billion in sales.[10]

The next immigration law of note – the Immigration Reform and Control Act (IRCA) of 1986 – legalized scores of undocumented people, but also established restrictive provisions for employers who hire them. IRCA also created a new classification of seasonal workers in the agricultural industry.

The following decade saw immigration changes that reflected the economic prosperity and reality of the time. In 1989, laws were enacted to help nurses immigrate to the U.S. to address a widespread shortage. The Immigration Act of 1990 increased total immigration, created separate categories based on family and employment, and instituted diversity visas for countries from which few people were emigrating.

The 1990s were also the start of a high-tech and dot com explosion in this country, with California's Silicon Valley at its epicenter. It witnessed the emergence of many of today's top employers. Yahoo! was co-founded in 1994 by Jerry Yang, who was born in Taiwan.

The multinational internet corporation boasted $4.8 billion in revenue in 2013 and more than 12,000 employees worldwide. In 2017, Yahoo! was acquired by Verizon Media.[11]

Paypal's co-founder Elon Musk was also born oversees, in South Africa. He came to the U.S. as a student in the early 1990s. He went on to found Tesla, starting a boom in the electric vehicle industry. He is also the creative visionary of other technological advancements including SpaceX.

Ebay's founder, Pierre Omidyar, was born in Paris to Iranian parents and moved to the U.S. when he was a child.

And of course, there's Google. Created in 1997 by Stanford University friends, Larry Page and Sergey Brin, and launched the following year, the company's name is now synonymous with internet search.[12] Brin was born in Russia in 1973 and immigrated to the U.S. with his family in 1979 to escape Jewish persecution.

Google[13], Ebay[14] and Paypal[15] combined supported well over 150,000 American jobs in 2020. Ukrainian native Jan Koum, together with Brian Acton, sold their mobile messaging application, WhatsApp, to Facebook for $19 billion in 2014. Founded in 2011 by Eric Yuan, a Chinese American, Zoom saw its annual revenue reach over $622 million in fiscal year 2020. It employs over 2,500 people.[16]

All of these companies, while U.S. based, are global household names. The Partnership for a New American Economy (PNAE), which advocates "the economic benefits of sensible immigration reform," reports that 40 percent of Fortune 500 companies were founded by immigrants or their children.[17]

The last significant immigration law passed by Congress was the Illegal Immigration Reform and Immigrant Responsibility Act (IIRIRA) of 1996. It focused mainly on enforcement and enacted sanctions for immigration violations, including for employers who fail to comply with regulations. In effect, the new law created harsh measures, though none specifically aimed at entrepreneurs.

Now, with technology advancements affecting every industry, from healthcare to agriculture, it is time to re-think where America wants to be in the next 10, 20 and even 100 years. The Covid-19 global pandemic, that started in 2020 and continues at the time of writing in March 2021, forced us to change the way we operate in our daily lives. It has affected how schools, hospitals, and restaurants function on a day-to-day basis. In fact, every industry has been so affected by this pandemic, that modernizing, and innovating have become urgent needs.

Archaic laws, remnants of an entirely different time and place, cannot accommodate our need for creative, highly educated and highly skilled workers. To do nothing will leave us in a state of mediocrity. So the question is: What kind of country do we want to be in the future?

2

AROUND THE GLOBE

P ivot to Canada. That was the message on a May 2013 billboard along Highway 101 between San Francisco and San Jose, the heart of Silicon Valley. The ad, boasting Canada's brand new Startup Visa, was a bold move to lure American-based entrepreneurs to our neighbor up north. Canada proclaimed this the first visa of its kind in the world. And it was a slap in the face to a dysfunctional American immigration system, seen as unfriendly to startup founders.

Ironically, Canada's Startup Visa legislation is based on the language of the Startup Visa Act of 2010, the U.S.' first attempt at such a measure, which was introduced and then died in the Congress.

Whereas Canada's startup visa program, launched in 2010, is up and running, recruiting talented skilled entrepreneurs, the U.S. version has not moved an inch. Various bipartisan measures have been introduced since, including within the 2013 comprehensive immigration reform bill. However, none passed into law.

In Canada, meanwhile, the Startup law[1] initially provided 2,750 visas to foreign entrepreneurs for each year of the five-year pilot program. Due to its success, Canada made it permanent in 2018.

Foreign nationals, with funding from Canadian venture capital firms, angel investor groups or business incubators that are included on a government-approved designated organizations' list can apply for immediate permanent residency.[2] Since the first edition of this book, the number of designated organizations has grown significantly.

Each entrepreneur must secure a minimum investment of $200,000 if the investment comes from designated Canadian venture capital funds, or $75,000 if it comes from a designated Canadian angel investor group. Canada issued its first visas to two Ukrainian entrepreneurs in July 2014 and as of January 2015, had issued a total of five. In 2019, about 510 visas were granted. While it was slow to take off, the program's success has earned it a permanent place in the immigration books and is definitely an example for others.

And like Canada, other countries are eager to attract entrepreneurs, enticing them with special visas and funding. Between 2012 and 2014, from the Americas to the Asian continent, several countries implemented new policies and programs to bring innovation and job creation within their borders. And since writing the first edition of this book, more countries have added the Startup Visas to their immigration options. One example is Startup Chile, which was created in 2010, the same year the U.S. Congress introduced the Startup Visa here. Chile offers a $40,000 grant for seed funding to qualified entrepreneurs from around the world. The unique government-funded program requires the foreign entrepreneur to teach Chilean youth about business and the companies generally hire two or three local citizens. The program has inspired much financial growth and job creation and has had other positive impacts.[3] The model has influenced the creation of 50 entrepreneurship programs across the world. Additionally, Malaysia, Brazil, Jamaica, Puerto Rico, Peru and South Korea directly replicated the Startup Chile model.[4]

In a desperate bid to boost employment following an economic meltdown, Ireland also created a Startup Entrepreneur program in April 2012. It was one of the first European countries to do so and aims to foster new enterprises, and the program applicant must have financial backing of no less than €75,000. Approved participants and their immediate families are allowed to enter Ireland on multi-entry visas and remain there for two years. Since its inception about two years ago, 21 visas have been granted.[5]

In 2012, the United Kingdom launched its Tier 1 Entrepreneur visa, which offers investors permanent residency if they invest £200,000 in a UK business. The program is part of a five-tier, points-based visa system that exists for those trying to immigrate to the UK. Tier 1 visas are aimed at entrepreneurs, investors and the very small number of people who qualify under what's known as the 'exceptional talent' visa category.

Also in 2014, New Zealand and Italy launched their own versions of the Startup Visa. The Netherlands also jumped on board, approving a Startup Visa in December 2014 and launching it in January 2015.

As of February 2021, the following countries have some form of a Startup Visa: UK, Denmark, Sweden, Ireland, Singapore, New Zealand, Australia, Germany, Italy, Chile, France, Thailand, Canada, Spain, Belgium, Portugal, Netherlands, Finland, Latvia, Austria, Estonia, Lithuania.

Although many of these new Startup Visas have their own limitations, they demonstrate an eagerness by a growing number of countries to embrace foreign entrepreneurs, while the U.S. remains mired in political gridlock. We make it easy for immigrants to acquire the best education here, but then practically force them to go elsewhere to put that knowledge to work. As stated by Vivek Wadhwa, "Gone are the days when the U.S. was the only land of opportunity and when entrepreneurs dreamed of being acquired by a Silicon Valley company. The bigger opportunities now lie in countries such as India, China and Brazil, and their entrepreneurs are becoming confident that they can take on Silicon Valley."[6]

Yet entrepreneurs still want to be in the U.S. The market is larger and businesses are relatively easy to open. Investors willing to take risks are more accessible. However, without the availability of a Startup Visa, we stand to lose talented people, and the opportunity to remain leaders in innovation and job creation. The American Bar Association, the U.S. Chamber of Commerce and the Partnership for a New American Economy are among the many organizations that back a Startup Visa. Lawmakers from both sides of the aisle also support one. Former New York City Mayor Michael Bloomberg summed it up this way: "When every other country wants the best and the brightest, we're trying to keep them out. It doesn't make a lot of sense... [T]he truth of the matter is we are sending the future overseas. We need people to start companies and create jobs. People who come from overseas are something like ... five times more likely to create jobs than people who are here... So we've got to do something about this."[7]

3

SQUARE PEGS IN ROUND HOLES

E very country wants to be home to the next founder of Facebook, Google or Microsoft. It's a race to the top that the U.S., for the most part, has been leading. But increasingly, entrepreneurs in the U.S. are finding themselves mired in outdated rules and regulations. One reason is because Congress has failed to act to address shortcomings in our laws. But another is because, like trying to force square pegs into round holes, our current visa options are not viable for most foreign entrepreneurs. I summarize the various options here and explain why they don't work well for startups.

EB-5 Investor Visa:

The current investor visa program, established in 1990, allows for immediate permanent residency for those who: (1) invest $1 million in any business in any part of the U.S. and generate 10 new full-time jobs; or (2) invest $500,000 in a Targeted Employment Area (TEA) and generate 10 new full-time jobs.[1] The law defines a targeted employment area as either rural or an area of high unemployment.

The EB-5 visa program has contributed significantly to the U.S. economy. A January 2018 economic impact report published by Western Washington University Center for Economic Business Research (CEBR) found that during the fiscal years of 2014 and 2015, the EB-5 program generated $11.2 billion in capital investment, supported 207,000 American jobs and generated $4.2 billion in tax revenue for federal, state and local governments -- all at no cost to the U.S. taxpayer.[2]

However, the EB-5 visa program is a poor fit for boot-strapped, hard-working, talented and creative entrepreneurs, who generally don't have that kind of money at their disposal. This visa is for the investor who is not interested in being the next Google founder, but wants to pour money into a safe and successful project that will allow him or her to fulfill the requirements to obtain a green card.

Incidentally, it is worth noting that Canada scrapped its EB-5 equivalent in 2013 because it was not deemed a job-generator, and was creating inequalities for Canadian citizens. In December 2014, however, it announced plans to launch a brand new program to allow only 50 high-net-worth immigrant investors annually to actually invest in startups, demonstrating that Canada is being creative in finding more ways to attract foreign investment.[3]

E-2 Treaty Investor Visa:

Citizens of countries with which the U.S. maintains a treaty of commerce and navigation – about 40 countries to date – can apply for an E-2 visa. Most recently, Israel was added to the list of countries.

It allows entrepreneurs to come to the U.S. with their families, if they have the financial wherewithal to operate a business here. This visa can be issued for up to five years at a time, with no limits on renewal, but on its own can never lead to legal permanent residency for its holders.

Like the EB-5, the E-2 benefits the economy by bringing capital infusion and creating jobs. But it has many limitations.

Because it's a non-immigrant visa, the holder can only reside in the U.S. as long as the business is active and profitable. Furthermore, not all countries maintain the required treaties with the U.S.,[4] therefore, the majority of graduates and high-skilled workers coming from India and mainland China are ineligible for an E-2. I have many clients who are otherwise eligible but cannot benefit from this visa because of their nationalities.

While the law does not specify the investment necessary to obtain an E-2 visa, it does state that a substantial amount of money should be invested.[5] Most immigration lawyers say the rule of thumb is to invest around $100,000 for a successful case, although lesser amounts have also qualified. As with the EB-5, most founders do not have that kind of money to invest in a business.

An additional problem: to qualify for an E-2 visa, an applicant must have at least 51 percent ownership in the business. However, if the ownership structure includes funding from investors, and especially if there are multiple founders, the foreign entrepreneur might see shares dwindle below 51 percent, preventing continued eligibility for this visa.

H-1B Employment Visa:

The H-1B visa is the workhorse of U.S. employment visas, easily the most popular and aimed specifically at skilled professionals who have earned at least a Bachelor's degree. Each year, 65,000 visas are issued to foreign-born people to work in any number of jobs – from computer programmers to high school teachers. An additional 20,000 are granted to those who hold a Master's degree from an American college or university and an unlimited number are granted to researchers, professors and other workers at American colleges, universities and certain research institutes. The H-1B is valid for six years. It is initially granted for three years and can be extended for another three. Beyond that, an applicant must have a green card application pending or approved to be able to remain in the country.

While this visa is the most widely used by U.S. employers to fill skilled-worker positions, for entrepreneurs seeking to start companies, it is not a particularly good fit.

Traditionally, the H-1B visa has not been used for the self-employed. However, in August 2011, U.S. Citizenship and Immigration Services (USCIS) announced a policy change to allow entrepreneurs to apply for H-1Bs through their own startup companies.[6] The company itself – not the entrepreneur – must file the petition and there must be evidence that the entrepreneur is an employee of the company. The policy has seen some success, but there are many problems with applying the H-1B to entrepreneurs.

Numerical limitation is the most obvious. The demand for H-1B visas is far greater than the supply. In April 2020 (for fiscal year 2021), for example, USCIS received 275,000 applications, more than triple the number of visas available. An entrepreneur growing a business cannot afford the uncertainty of such a lottery. It must be noted that the Trump administration made some procedural changes to the process in April 2020, allowing H-1B lottery applications to be submitted electronically for a nominal registration fee of $10.00. Only if selected in the lottery would one need to prepare and mail in a completed application. Admittedly, it was one of the few good decisions surrounding immigration that emerged during the Trump years as it allowed for a cost and time efficient process of entering the lottery. In turn, it also allowed USCIS to conduct the lottery in a speedy manner. It helps to explain, in part why there was a significant increase in submissions from prior years. We can expect such demand going forward.

There are other requirements of the H-1B visa that make it inefficient for startups. For example, the company must prove the owner's salary will be at the prevailing wage, defined as the wages and benefits paid to the majority of workers in the largest city in each county.

Because technology wages are high, the prevailing wage in that industry is substantial. The typical startup company, struggling during its fledgling years to stay afloat, is not always able, financially, to accommodate this provision.

While USCIS has always challenged practically every aspect of H-1B petitions generally, resulting in denials, even for obviously approvable cases, the Trump administration took that scrutiny to unprecedented levels resulting in the highest denial rates in history.[7]

Another problem created by the Trump administration leaves us with greater uncertainty about the program's future. Just before Trump left office in January 2021, his administration issued a final rule on H-1B prevailing wages.[8] It essentially gives those with the highest wages preference in the lottery process. There are four levels of wages when assessing the appropriate wage for an H-1B worker, starting from entry level to very experienced.

The new wage-based lottery would instantly eliminate the entry level positions and cause an imbalance in how employers can afford and retain talent. Immediately upon taking office, the Biden administration delayed implementation of this rule. It allowed lawyers like me to breathe a sigh of relief because the change would have affected almost all of our clients.

It should be noted that the H-1B visa program is used by almost every industry in which there are professionals – doctors, lawyers, architects, teachers and of course the engineers in and out of the technology industry. Entrepreneurs can be in any of these industries and would absolutely be impacted by the wage-based rule if it ultimately goes into effect. We'll have to wait and see what the new administration does. (Follow our blog at Watson Immigration Law[9] to keep informed on this issue.)

Another problem with using H-1B for entrepreneurs is that the job description of the founder's H-1B position must match precisely the tasks described in the Department of Labor's job library. For example, a software engineer must perform all the duties of a software engineer, and nothing else. However, a founder will be wearing many other hats, in addition to software engineer and therefore, a narrow interpretation of the H-1B job description will pose a problem. In other words, the founder could be performing all the duties of a software engineer as well as the duties as a founder, and that could lead to a denial.

L-1 Intra-Company Transferee:

In an era of globalization, the L-1 is an often-used visa that allows certain personnel – usually a manager or executive, as well employees with special knowledge – to transfer to the U.S. from a foreign office or an affiliate of a U.S. company. To qualify, the foreign office must be related to the U.S. office with the same or similar ownership and the employee must have worked in that foreign office for at least one of the past three years. The L-1 has been a vehicle for many businesses to establish a presence in the U.S.

The L-1 visa, though, comes with its own unique problems. Requiring foreign and U.S. companies to have a qualifying relationship – as a parent firm with a subsidiary, affiliate or branch office – is perhaps the most problematic. An entrepreneur in another country seeking to start a new company in the U.S. would most likely not have an affiliation with a U.S. company, let alone meet the one-year working requirement.

But beyond that, almost all L-1 visas for new companies have recently faced increased scrutiny for fear of fraud. In 2013, the Department of Homeland Security's Office of Inspector General issued a lengthy report[10] outlining ten broad recommendations, including additional screening and site visits for newly established offices in the U.S. Since then, we have seen more scrutiny of applications.[11] This visa simply does not fit the circumstances of most startup founders.

O-1 Extraordinary Ability:

The O-1 visa, dubbed the genius visa, is reserved for those who can prove they are at the top echelon of their profession and are indeed extraordinary. It's frequently used by celebrities and past holders have included British journalist Piers Morgan, who replaced Larry King on CNN in 2010, and John Oliver, one of my favorite talk show hosts who happens also to be British and who hosts Last Week Tonight on HBO. Increasingly, this temporary work visa is being used more often for high-tech entrepreneurs. Some requirements include proof the applicant has acquired national or international acclaim, mention in the media or a significant contribution in their field, such as finding the cure for some deadly disease. A full list can be found at 8 CFR §214.2(o).

However, the standard for meeting such a high burden of proof is extremely difficult, and most new entrepreneurs cannot do so for several reasons. Many are upcoming or recent college graduates who will not have had the career or life experiences to reach the highest levels of their profession.

In other circumstances, they may have had long careers at companies where they focused on a special service or product. And while they may have expertise in that one thing, they will not have had the opportunity to develop their careers in the way the O-1 visa mandates. Thus, it is not always appropriate for entrepreneurs.

EB-1 Extraordinary Ability:

While the O-1 is only a temporary work visa, the EB-1 visa is for permanent residency and can lead to a green card. The requirements mirror those of the O-1 visa. And for the same reasons, it also is not a good fit for entrepreneurs. While it can be used when the startup founder has received much public acknowledgement for raising large sums of money and creating many jobs, that often is still not enough to meet the requirements for this visa.

National Interest Waiver:

At the same time it announced the self-employed H-1B policy change in 2011, USCIS unveiled a plan to broaden the scope of the immigrant visa category. Known as the National Interest Waiver (NIW), it was intended to help entrepreneurs file petitions for legal permanent residency, or green cards – something the USCIS change on its own could not do.[12] The NIW is an application process to obtain a green card in the U.S. without the need for a family petition or offer of employment. It has no legal definition. At the time of writing the first edition of the book, USCIS relied on a 1998 Administrative Appeals Office precedent decision *In Re. New York State*

Department of Transportation which sets forth a three-pronged test for evaluating requests for the NIW.[13]

First, the area of work must be of "substantial intrinsic merit." Second, the benefit must be "national in scope." And finally, the applicant must be able to prove that in their absence the "national interest would be adversely affected." In other words, the applicant would have to show that their work impacts the nation and that the interest of America would be harmed by not allowing them to stay.

This was a challenging standard to start with, but an even bigger one for entrepreneurs. How can one prove that being unable to stay in the U.S. would be harmful to the country? This became a special obstacle as the Obama administration tried to carve out entrepreneur-friendly policies.

In December 2016, the Administrative Appeals Office issued a ruling in what has become a precedent-setting case, *In Re. Matter of Dhanasar*.[14] Dhanasar recognized the challenges of the standards imposed on NIW applicants and set a new one that primarily turned the third prong into an affirmative action.

Under the new framework, an NIW may be approved if, (1) the foreign national's proposed endeavor has both substantial merit and national importance; (2) the foreign national is well-positioned to advance the proposed endeavor; (3) on balance, it would be beneficial to the United States to waive the requirements of a job offer and thus of a labor certification. *Dhanasar* sets some clear factors to consider for the third prong, making it more reasonable to meet the requirements.

Entrepreneurs welcomed this policy adjustment when it was made because the process in place to petition for an employment-based green card for H-1B workers, on its own, cannot be applied to the self-employed. Why? Under current law, traditional employers petitioning for a green card for their immigrant employees must demonstrate a good-faith effort to first recruit American workers for the jobs. Obviously, entrepreneurs starting their own businesses can't prove they are trying to recruit for their own position.

An additional problem with the NIW is that the waiting time for obtaining a green card through this path can be long. It falls within a visa-granting category where the wait can be decades for citizens of India, China, Mexico and the Philippines. Therefore, a large number of people will not be able to benefit from the rule change as was intended.

Each of the above visas work well for certain cases and they've resulted in many foreigners being able to stay in the U.S., work here and in some cases start businesses. But those instances are too few and the process is too tortured. These visas are ill-suited for the immigrant who wants to start and grow a new business and, in some instances, secure funding from investors.

What's more, none takes into consideration that increasingly, in an era of high-speed internet when technology is cheap and easy to access, someone with a brilliant idea doesn't always need a significant amount of money to get a startup off the ground. Facebook and Google are examples of such success, started by founders during college and graduate school, respectively. Immigration policies must reflect that, too.

4

PITY THE STARTUP FOUNDER

On January 8, 2010, Donald Neufeld, associate director of
service center operations of USCIS, issued a memo imposing
drastic restrictions on employment-based visa petitions.[1] His action
was triggered by a 2008 USCIS report, *H-1B Benefit Fraud and
Compliance Assessment*, which found that 13 percent of H-1B petitions filed by employers were fraudulent. Neufeld's memo flagged as
a fraud indicator, for example, those employers with fewer than 25
employees and less than $10 million in gross revenue. The study also
found a lack of adherence to the job descriptions outlined in Department of Labor guidelines. In seeking to address these problems,
Neufeld imposed strict burdens on proving an employer-employee
relationship for H-1B petitions, namely that the employer has a right
to hire and fire the employee and that it controls his or her work. The
15-page fraud report affected all employers – big and small.

Coming on the heels of what in the industry has become known as
the Neufeld Memo, was a set of guidelines from the USCIS that, for
the first time, allowed startup founders to apply for H-1B visas. Even
sole proprietors could apply.

But while initially applauded, the challenge of these changes, taken together, was immediately obvious. The guidelines were predicated upon the Neufeld memo and required startup companies applying for H-1B visas to produce evidence that the founder's employment was controlled by the company. A board of directors could be sufficient to prove such control.

Proving that the employer controls the work of the employee when the founder is both employer and employee can be tricky. The USCIS expects an onerous amount of corporate documentation, including articles of incorporation, board meeting minutes, shareholder agreements, stock ledgers, etc. This extreme burden often results in denial of the case.

The case of one client, whose real name, like all others I mention in this chapter, has been changed to protect his identity, illustrates the problem. Todd Leahry, a Canadian citizen, is co-founder of a company that employs seven full-time American workers and has helped create several indirect jobs by virtue of those who use and sell his product. Todd, his U.S.-born partner and their company have garnered wide praise from throughout the tech industry.

In early 2011, when his company made the initial filing for his H-1B visa, the Neufeld Memo was in play, but the USCIS self-employment guidelines had not yet been released. So it wasn't necessary for Todd to disclose that he was part owner of the company; policy did not require it. The employer-employee relationship still applied and in Todd's case, was proven with relevant documents.

When Todd sought to extend his H-1B two years later, he filed a petition just like the first one. However, by then, the self-employment guidelines were in force and Todd's ownership interest in his firm needed to be specifically disclosed to USCIS - but wasn't.

The final question for renewing Todd's visa centered on the relationship between him and his firm. The USCIS believed that it was discovering for the first time that Todd was a co-founder of his company. Suddenly, he faced the real possibility of having to leave the U.S. because the government falsely believed he may have been trying to hide his relationship with his company. It was at this stage I was brought in to help file the response.

As a team, we brainstormed the type of documentation he would be able to provide. We decided to give the government many internal and otherwise confidential documents to demonstrate he was always given direction in his work and he was not the decision maker. We submitted emails, client contracts, employee information, payroll evidence, references and much more. It was a burdensome and challenging request, but in the end we prevailed.

The example illustrates how startups are sometimes treated in the H-1B context and the difficulties that can arise. In 2021, this treatment is still the same. If anything, H-1B visas for self-employment are generally more challenging because of the restrictive policies put in place by the Trump administration. The 'Buy American and Hire American' executive order (EO 13788) signed in April 2017 led to substantial across-the-board changes in adjudication standards for employment-based immigration applications. New policies were issued that resulted in increased rates of requests for evidence (RFE), and denials. As practitioners, we saw novel and burdensome requests, nitpicking every aspect of the application. For the first time, we saw USCIS use an entry-level wage as an opening to send such burdensome requests even in the strongest of cases. While President Biden revoked the BAHA executive order upon taking office, in early 2021, its impact still remains.

By their very nature, startup companies operate leanly. Their founders often work around the clock to ensure their enterprises are successful – that employees are properly supervised and clients are happy.

But rather than using his energy to build the business, Todd had to spend a great deal of time anxious and worried about providing enough of the right kind of information to respond to the government.

During this period, he suffered losses both emotionally and financially. As a result, his business, partners, employees, and clients were all put in limbo. He faced the real possibility of having to up-root his wife and family from the U.S., a proposition he knew would be so upsetting to his wife, he kept it a secret from her for as long as he could.

It makes no sense to create an environment of inefficiency at a crucial time when an entrepreneur is trying to get his business off the ground. One should not have to feel defensive for founding a company; it should be a source of pride. Luckily, in Todd's case, we were able to successfully demonstrate that his employment was controlled by his company. But many founders are not so lucky.

Too many end up cut off from the companies they helped to create by our policies and laws, which are often disconnected from the demands of today's modern world where globalization has made nations, economies and people more connected than ever.

While Todd was able to eventually continue to work for his firm with an H-1B visa, Kumar Patel, a citizen of India, faced a different outcome. Kumar had come to the U.S. as a student almost 20 years earlier, completed his Bachelor's and Master's degrees in engineering, and went on to work at some of the top Fortune 500 companies in the country, including Microsoft. Microsoft had petitioned for a green card on his behalf.

However, the wait for a green card to become available for someone from India currently exceeds 11 years and sadly, Kumar is still waiting.[2] In the meantime, he continues to nurture ideas for creating products that could literally change people's lives. He wants to start his own company, but can't because he's stuck in a holding pattern waiting for a green card.

First, there is no suitable visa for him to start his own company, other than the self-employed H-1B, which is too risky for him to try. Second, there is no mechanism to transfer his pending green card application to a startup company. So, he continues his daily life working at Microsoft, but dreaming of the day he can create his own company. Sadly, because of his age, he may not get the opportunity to do so in his lifetime.

Some would-be entrepreneurs end up becoming so frustrated, they give up and return home, where they try to develop there, what they are unable to here. That was the case with Jamal Jay, a bright and talented young man from India. Upon graduation from a U.S. college, Jamal worked under an H-1B visa for Microsoft, which diligently applied for his green card. Like Kumar, Jamal also became a victim to the waiting game. He transferred his H-1B to another company, but that did not address his desire to start his own company.

In addition to his own frustrations, his wife – a professional woman in her own right – was not allowed to work. At the time, holders of H-4 visas, for the spouses of H-1B workers, were not, by law, permitted to work in this country. New policies instituted by President Obama's Executive Action would later change that.

But by then, mounting frustrations had compelled the couple to return to India, where Jamal launched a successful startup. He may or may not return to the U.S. But what a shame that we are educating bright, promising young people who end up taking their education and training elsewhere?

And it's not just people from the Asian continent, either. Joey Grayson is a Canadian citizen who also worked at Microsoft on an H-1B visa before teaming up with friends to launch a startup. To be clear, Joey did not have a huge stake in this company – a negligible 2 percent.

He resigned from Microsoft and returned to Canada around the time they were trying to get the business off the ground. Since employment visas are employer specific, we needed to find an option that would allow the new company to sponsor Joey so he could return to the U.S. The question was how to get his visa through a startup firm, in which he owns some stock?

Citizens of Canada are eligible to apply for what's known as Treaty NAFTA (TN) visas, approval for which can be relatively quick and easy if all the requirements are met. Generally, the TN visa applicant cannot be self-employed. In this case, Joey's company was too new and USCIS viewed it with suspicion.

So, Joey's initial application was denied. He was stuck in Canada and separated from the business. After a few months, with a little revenue stream and more substantial finances in the business, the TN was approved – but for only a year, which is not much time.

The business was gaining ground and growing stronger in a short period of time, but Joey's visa timeline was coming to an end. At this time, around 2009, self-employed H-1Bs were not yet specifically allowed, but the business also needed more sustainable revenue for a successful application, as a prevailing wage is the foundation of the petition. The business was poised to receive funding from investors and Joey's immigration status was crucial to securing that investment. In the end, he married his long-term girlfriend – a U.S. citizen – which solved his immigration problem.

But while Joey was lucky that the love of his life was an option for his immigration problem, matrimony is not an option for everyone.

Since Congress had proven incapable of enacting new legislation, the USCIS, under the leadership of then-Director of USCIS Alejandro Mayorkas (who was confirmed as Secretary of the Department of Homeland Security in February 2021), created a new initiative in 2012 called the Entrepreneur in Residence (EIR) program. Its aim was to help immigrant entrepreneurs – and they welcomed it. The program brought together immigration adjudication officers and startup experts with fresh ideas for working within the current legal framework.[3] It also created a web portal that allowed entrepreneurs to assess which visa categories would be appropriate for them. Under the program, officers were trained in modern-day entrepreneurial issues, allowing them to make more informed decisions. (It should be noted that the Trump administration silently did away with the EIR program.)

This training was key at the time, as it allowed officers to consider USCIS' policy changes for self-employed H-1Bs as well as the National Interest Waivers (NIW) for entrepreneurs. In essence, the EIR team at USCIS was trained to adjudicate all entrepreneur cases with a keen understanding of how startups operate.

For some entrepreneurs, the addition of the EIR team, together with the new, updated policy guidance, was a reprieve – albeit temporary. A Canadian citizen born in Korea, Alan Leffert was a genius in his own right. He, too, worked at Microsoft and resigned to start his own company. He wanted to change the way certain high-end consumer products sold online. And when the USCIS allowed self-employed H-1Bs, he became a program pioneer.

He had to prove his business partner was going to control his work and have the ability to hire or fire him. Documentation to that effect had to be created, including for Alan to relinquish voting rights in the business. He was lucky enough to get an H-1B with his new company in a matter of days, thanks in part to the EIR officers' understanding of startups. While he, his partner and venture capitalists invested heavily in the company, the fast-growing startup was still having cash flow problems, common for startups that are scaling up. Maintaining the terms of his H-1B status – that he be paid a prevailing wage of $100,000 a year – was a real struggle. It's one of many reasons the H-1B is not well suited for startups. Until the firm's revenue stream stabilizes, finances are always tight.

What's more, Alan needed permanent residency to ensure investors could rely on him to continue running the business. His H-1B timeline was limited, as were his green card options because he had ownership in his company.

As discussed before, the traditional process of parlaying an H-1B visa into a green card – also known as the permanent labor certification application and commonly referred to as PERM, works against people like him. It is why USCIS, in allowing self-employed H-1B petitions in 2011, also provided guidelines for the NIW for entrepreneurs to prove their work would have a national impact in order to qualify for green cards.

While that would have been the most practical and sensible option for him, there was no certainty his petition would have been approved. While his company might well have been able to prove his new method of online sales does indeed have broad, national influence, it takes time for a startup to become established and spread its business impact. Alan's business had 15 full-time employees. While job creation is what the NIW for entrepreneurs generally seeks, the arguments for national intrinsic merit and national scope – the standards used – have a very high bar. (Please see chapter 8 for legal updates to NIW.)

Unfortunately, since publishing this book in 2015, Alan's company folded and he had to leave the U.S. To ensure immigration requirements were met, he gave up more shares than he wanted. As a result, his partner had more voting rights than he did, even though the company was Alan's vision. The imbalance in the relationship affected the business, leading ultimately to its failure.

Another temporary success story of the EIR program is Norman Romanio. A Canadian citizen, Norman was selected to participate in Techstars Seattle, a 13-week mentorship-driven program to accelerate startup companies. After he graduated from the Techstars program in the U.S. in 2008, he obtained an H-1B visa through his company.

This was before the Neufeld Memo and the USCIS self-employment policy change. Norman was one of several co-founders of the company, but not its CEO and didn't have to disclose ownership.

Two years later, the most successful of his products and assets were acquired by a large company, likely for several million dollars. This is the dream of any startup founder. As part of the deal, Norman worked for the company that acquired the product. In fact, thanks to his product, the acquiring company was named one of the fastest-growing tech companies in New York. It generated millions of dollars in revenue and created almost 300 jobs.

By 2013, however, Norman was coming to the end of his term with the acquiring company and decided to revive the original firm that started it all.

Generally cautious of fraud, USCIS conducts thorough checks of companies' documentation to verify authenticity and ensure employers can afford to pay prevailing wages to their H-1B employees. The trouble for Norman was that the initial company had been dormant for some time, with no financial activity. Typically, this is a death knell for an H-1B petition. I came into the picture at this stage to assess how we could re-apply for the H-1B through a company unlikely to pass the fraud smell-test.

After assessing the conditions, I decided to trust the EIR program and its officers to recognize a genius startup founder. Instead of hiding the dormancy of the company, which would come out later anyway and seem even more suspicious, I decided to lay all the cards on the table.

I explained how talented Norman was, describing the revenue he had generated so far and the jobs he helped create in the U.S. I explained that given the chance again, Norman would be able replicate the model and continue to be an asset in the U.S. The trust worked and an EIR startup-trained adjudicator approved his H-1B petition.

But now Norman faced the green card issue. We strategized over whether to apply for the NIW. The unpredictability and inconsistency of adjudicating these cases and the lack of policy guidance – even with EIR officers involved – left him undecided as to whether he should apply or not. He wanted time to think about it and at this point, my representation of him came to an end. So, I don't know the end of his story.

This unpredictability means that we immigration attorneys are often sifting through a number of visa types to see which would be the right fit for our clients. In one recent case, it appeared the E-2 treaty visa would be that fit.

To qualify for it, one must first be a citizen of a country on the U.S. Treaty Countries list.[4] One must own at least 51% of the business. And one must demonstrate that his or her own funds are at risk. Though the law does not specify a minimum amount of investment, the rule of thumb is $100,000. Additionally, two founders from the same treaty country may apply under the same entity as 50% owners.

This doesn't leave any possibility of taking on investors, and is impossible if there are three co-founders. Even more challenging is the situation when founders are from different countries. That was the case with two recent clients who were citizens of two European countries. Fortunately for both, they were each from a treaty country, or the story may have had an altogether different ending.

They were both working on one startup while in Europe. But that startup, for reasons related to not having sufficient U.S. physical presence and financing yet, was not in a position to support an H-1B, nor was the timing right to apply for one in the once-a-year lottery. While we wanted to apply for an E-2 visa, they had already raised significant amount of funds and neither would qualify for an E-2 with the shares that they held. Because angel and venture capital investors also owned shares in the business, it meant my clients' shares were less than the legally required minimum amount of 51%. It should be noted that in some instances, 50-50 shares can work, but both investors must be from the same country.

In this situation, we needed the skillful advice of a corporate attorney on how to structure the company. After many meetings and brainstorming, we had no choice but to apply for individual E-2 applications for which they each had to reinvest in their separate companies, and obtain visas based on those separate entities.

At the time, the Trump Administration's Buy American and Hire American executive order had already made adverse and restrictive updates to the E-2 policies. While one founder was able to get a visa from one European embassy, the other was denied. The person denied was told by the U.S. consular officer to enter the U.S. on a B-1 business visa, get the business further established and then apply. The consular officer then issued a one year B-1 visa and my client followed the officer's guidance. However, Trump's policies also included executive orders on border security[5] which had resulted in extra scrutiny at airports. After a brief trip out of the country a few months into his B-1 visa, the client, upon his return, was interrogated at length at the airport. He was lucky to be allowed to enter the U.S. then, but was only given a few weeks to stay. Customs and Border Protection officers at the airport told him he should have entered with an E-2 visa instead.

As you can imagine, this was quite frustrating and infuriating. The consular office didn't give him an E-2 and the CBP officer gave him a hard time for not having an E-2. Eventually, we were able to secure the visa but not without a lot of stress. And during this time, the client lost valuable time, energy, funds and opportunities for the business because he had to deal with immigration issues.

There are many other stories of clients facing similar barriers in the E-2, O-1 and L-1A contexts as well.

It should be noted that during the Trump administration, the EIR unit became all but defunct and the administration also removed the EIR portal for entrepreneurs. As we settle into the Biden administration with Secretary Mayorkas at the helm of DHS, my hope is that the EIR unit will be revived.

For each of the people I mention in the above cases, and no doubt countless others, a Startup Visa would have been ideal. Visa requirements would have set forth guidelines for issues like jobs created, revenue generated, and funds raised. The founders would have been freed up to run their businesses. In the current economic crisis, don't we want such talented people?

5

LEGISLATIVE HISTORY

W hile the story of the entrepreneurial immigrant is not new, it wasn't until 2009 that the first concept of the Startup Visa was introduced in Congress[1] as part of a bill combined with other immigration issues. The current governor of Colorado Jared Polis,[2] who was a congressman at the time, worked together with Brad Feld, his co-founder of Techstars, and others, to formulate the vision. You can learn about the historic details of the inception and thought process in Brad Feld's own voice in the accompanying podcast series to this book, on my podcast "Tahmina Talks Immigration."[3]

Inspired by the above bill and a 2009 essay titled 'The Founder Visa'[4] written by the co-founder of Y-Combinator Paul Graham, lawmakers finally introduced a standalone Startup Visa bill in 2010. This time, Congress created a path specifically designed for international founders to obtain legal permanent status here. Since then, lawmakers have introduced several major bills authorizing a Startup Visa program. None has passed.

Former Senators John Kerry, D-Mass., and Richard Lugar, R-Ind., introduced the first one, S. 3029, with the aim of driving job creation and increasing America's global competitiveness. It would allow immigrant entrepreneurs to receive a two-year conditional immigrant visa if they could show that a qualified American investor was willing to dedicate a significant sum – a minimum of $250,000 – to the immigrant's startup venture and create a certain number of jobs. It would also create a new visa category for immigrant entrepreneurs, called EB-6, borrowing from the current EB-5 visa category, which permits foreign nationals who invest at least $1 million in a U.S. project, thereby creating 10 jobs, to obtain a green card. Although more than 160 venture capitalists from across the country endorsed the senators' proposal, the legislation never made it out of the Senate Judiciary Committee, where it died at the end of the 111th Congress.

Another attempt to enact Startup legislation came the following year, when Senators Lugar and Kerry, along with Senator Mark Udall, a Democrat from Colorado, reintroduced the legislation. The Startup Visa Act of 2011, S. 565, was an expanded version of the original. In addition to many key provisions spelled out in the original bill, this new version sought to broaden the potential pool of eligible immigrants to include those already here on H-1B visas, as well as entrepreneurs living outside the U.S. It also established new visa options for foreign entrepreneurs already living in the U.S. on E-2 visas as well as for entrepreneurs living abroad, setting forth conditions for each that included investment in their company, revenue generation and job creation. Unfortunately, this bill, too, never made it out of the Judiciary Committee.

In May 2012, Startup Act 2.0 was introduced by Sen. Jerry Moran, R-Kan. The legislation, S. 3217, called for a STEM visa to allow graduates in the fields of science, technology, engineering and math, to stay in the U.S. and start their own companies. The bill also proposed an entrepreneur visa and elimination of per-country caps for employment-based immigration. It died shortly after introduction.

In February the following year, Senator Moran again, along with Sens. Mark Warner, D-Va., Chris Coons, D-Del., and Roy Blunt, R-Mo., introduced the Startup Act 3.0, S. 310, to create both an entrepreneur and a STEM visa. The Entrepreneur Visa would allow entrepreneurs to enter and stay in the country, launch businesses and create jobs.

The STEM Visa would allow U.S.-educated foreign students, with an advance degree in any STEM field, to receive a green card. But this bill also stalled. It is this same bill that was reintroduced in January 2015 as The Startup Act, S.181.

Senate Bill 744:

Amid great anticipation and much fanfare, a bipartisan comprehensive immigration reform measure – the Border Security, Economic Opportunity and Immigration Modernization Act – was introduced in the Senate in April 2013. The centerpiece of the massive bill, and perhaps its most controversial component, sought to create a legal path for those in the country unlawfully.

But it seemed to have something for everyone – including entrepreneurs. The bill incorporated many of the provisions of Startup Act 3.0, including two new immigrant and non-immigrant visa categories for entrepreneurs.

The bill established requirements for this visa, called Invest Visa, based on jobs created and either funds raised from investors or revenue generated by the company. It also granted a preference to STEM graduates.

The Invest Visa provisions in the bill were seen as a creative solution to allow entrepreneurs to test their models before applying for green cards. The visa would be applicable to all industries, not just technology. I believe it is a good idea to have both temporary and permanent visa options as it would allow the government to assess the success of the business during the temporary visa stage before granting permanent residency. In addition, a temporary visa is generally processed more quickly, which enables the entrepreneur to enter the U.S. and start work immediately.

In the end, after much debate and analysis from nearly every sector, S. 744 passed by the then Democrat-controlled Senate in June 2013 – a historic win given that no immigration bill had passed that chamber in decades. However, it died in the then Republican-controlled House.

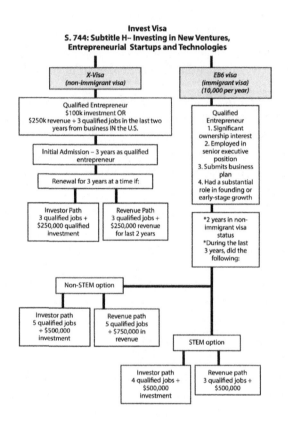

The Invest Visa Provisions

Entrepreneur Visa
SKILLS Visa Act (HR 2131)

EB-8 Immigrant Visa
10,000 visas per year

| Venture capital-backed start-up entrepreneurs | Treaty investors |

Requirements:	Requirements:
New commercial enterprise	Must be on E2 Visa
Secured at least $500,000 from qualified VC OR $100,000 from qualified angel investor	Maintained E2 for at least 10 years
	Maintain at least 5 full-time jobs for a minimum of 10 years

Permanent green card

Conditional green card

Next requirements:

2-year period beginning on the date on which the visa is issued
Created 5 f/t jobs;

and

Raised additional $1 million capital investment
or
$1 million revenue

Permanent green card

Skills Visa

39

About the same time the Senate was debating S. 744, another startup bill was introduced in the House. H.R. 2131 – the Supplying Knowledge-based Immigrants and Lifting Levels of STEM Visas Act or SKILLS Visa Act, sponsored by Rep. Darrell Issa, R-Calif.[5] Unlike the measure in the Senate, Issa's bill did not have much support. Rep. Zoe Lofgren, D-Calif., said the bill takes a "zero sum approach" to high-skilled immigration reform and "gives to some by only taking away from others."[6] It was reported out of the House Judiciary Committee in July 2013 but didn't go any further.

H.R. 2131 includes provisions for a Startup Visa, called the "Entrepreneur Visa" or EB-8 – a two-pronged instrument, aimed on one hand at entrepreneurs with venture capital backing and on the other, at foreigners already in the country on an E-2 Treaty Investor visa.

While the bill attempts to address the lack of a visa for entrepreneurs, the provisions will not accomplish the intended goal. For one thing it establishes financial thresholds that are way too high. It's nearly impossible for people to secure funding from a U.S. investor without already being in the U.S. And even if they can obtain the initial funding, it is virtually impossible for the majority of people to secure an additional $1 million in funding or revenue generation in only two years. A venture capital firm or angel investor, who has already invested in the company, will no doubt be vested in its success. But such success can take time to observe and nurture. Without making an assessment of the ongoing business needs, it is unlikely that an investor will put an additional $1 million into the business.

Commercial Enterprise:

Another fault of this legislation is regarding those who can take advantage of the second prong, where one must already be in the

U.S. on an E-2 visa to apply. As a result, only a small pool of people might be able to qualify.

These provisions are too stringent. Such provisions would give the appearance of a Startup Visa only.

In October 2013, a Democratic coalition in the House, led by Rep. Joe Garcia, D-Fla., introduced H.R.15, the Border Security, Economic Opportunity, and Immigration Modernization Act of 2013. I was proud that my home-state Congresswoman, Suzan Delbene, D-Wash., co-sponsored the bill and took a lead role in its politics. It was the House's answer to and a tweaked version of Senate bill 744, which Republican House leaders had refused to take up. The House version replaced some of the provisions contained in the Senate bill, primarily those having to do with border security, with some they believed would be more acceptable to Republicans. It retained the entrepreneur visas contained in the Senate version. Still, it didn't get very far. While it was hoped to be a good compromise, the politics of the day simply didn't favor comprehensive immigration reform.

Since the first publication of this book and since the above listed history, a few other bills have been introduced in Congress.

Rep. Zoe Lofgren (D-CA) introduced the EB-JOBS Act in 2015 which created a path for permanent residence if foreign-born entrepreneurs raised a certain level of funds or created at least five permanent full-time jobs. Entrepreneurs could self-fund their investment also. The National Foundation for American Policy estimated[7] the bill could have created 1 million to 3.2 million jobs over the course of a decade if it had become law.[8]

Others bills included S.3510 Attracting and Retaining Entrepreneurs Act introduced by Sen. Flake (R-AZ) in 2016; H.R. 2577 Jobs in America Act sponsored by Rep. (now senator) Sinema (D-AZ-9),

Rep. Valadao (R-CA-21), Rep. Polis (D-CO-2), and others; and the Startup Acts in 2017 and 2019 by Sen. Moran (R-KS), Sen. Warner (D-VA), Sen. Blunt (R-MO) and Sen. Klobuchar (D-MN).

Most notably, at the time of writing this second edition, the Biden-Harris administration's sweeping immigration reform bill U.S. Citizenship Act 2021 was introduced in February 2021. It starkly lacks a Startup Visa provision.

Senate vs. House:

Why does it matter now? The political and economic landscape of America has changed significantly since the first edition of this book. The aftermath of the Trump presidency has given rise to political desire and public approval for immigration reform. Additionally, the economic hardship brought on by the Covid-19 pandemic exacerbates the need to create jobs quickly. The Startup Visa is an opportunity to do so.

But more importantly, the legislative history above, demonstrates real opportunities for passing a Startup Visa – and the colossal failings on the part of Congress each time. It shows that we have a foundation and language that we can build on for future bills. The future however, is now.

6

CHANGES WITHOUT CONGRESS
PART I
THE INTERNATIONAL ENTREPRENEUR RULE

R hetoric and red-tape. Both are hindering immigration policies that could benefit entrepreneurs. As Former New York Mayor and former presidential candidate Michael Bloomberg stated, "[o]ur nation cannot afford to wait for Washington to get its act together and pass comprehensive immigration reform. There is too much at stake. Our economy demands that we take immediate action on the most urgent – and politically attainable – reform: making it easier for job creators to come and stay here."[1]

As the Biden Administration picks up the reins in Washington after four grueling and difficult years under Donald Trump, we are in a moment that is ripe and ready for change. The public desires it and we have an administration willing and eager to implement positive changes in our immigration laws. We also might learn from the Trump administration's fearless action on immigration. While Trump and his advisers sought to limit immigration through executive action, the Biden administration could use the same authority to advance policies to make us the welcoming country we need to be.

At the time of this writing, the U.S. Citizenship Act 2021, an immigration reform bill, has been introduced. Congress, meanwhile, is strategically voting on piecemeal bills. The measure lacks provisions for a Startup Visa. It is hard to know if and when a standalone Startup Visa Act will be introduced and if introduced, whether it would pass a divided Congress. That's why President Biden and his administration need to keep moving forward with executive action on solutions for immigrant entrepreneurs.

It's not a new strategy. In November 2014, President Obama, citing the failure of Congress to act on immigration reform, announced a series of executive actions to end the rhetoric and specifically include immigrant entrepreneurs in the nation's immigration system.

Using the provision known as the "significant public benefit" prong contained in existing immigration laws, his administration introduced a new program called the International Entrepreneur Rule (IER). The Immigration and Nationality Act section 212(d)(5) allows the Secretary of Homeland Security to use his discretion to parole any alien applying for admission into the U.S. temporarily for urgent humanitarian reasons or significant public benefit. In immigration jargon, 'parole' means permission to enter the United States.

The purpose of the proposed regulation was to "increase and enhance entrepreneurship, innovation, and job creation" in the U.S. The parole would be issued at an officer's discretion and on a case-by-case basis to start-up entities able to demonstrate that they would provide a significant public benefit to the United States.[2] In other words, the startup founders would have to demonstrate that they have or will create new jobs for Americans and raise funds or revenue.

The new rule would allow researchers, inventors and co-founders of startup companies who have raised money from U.S. investors and created or have the potential to create jobs, to enter the U.S. on a case-by-case basis. It was a welcome and inventive solution for entrepreneurs who otherwise would not be permitted to come to the U.S.

Since writing the first edition of this book, I spent significant time between 2015 and 2017 advocating for, writing about and presenting on the International Entrepreneur Rule (IER).

This is how it unfolded:

After the failed attempt of immigration reform in Congress, President Obama and his administration, in 2014, sought public comments on various ideas to retool immigration, including on the IER. I personally saw it as a great opportunity and spent a lot of time submitting ideas on Federal Register Doc 2014-30641. On August 26, 2016, the administration introduced creative and clear rules that would allow IER founders to start companies in the U.S.[3] Below is an FAQ I drafted during that time for easy understanding of those rules. The comment period ended in October 2016[4] and the final rule was published on January 16, 2017, with an implementation date of July 17, 2017.[5]

However, when Trump won the election and was inaugurated in January 2017, it was evident that he was on a mission to undo everything that President Obama had achieved. He set his sight on IER and added a freeze to the regulation on January 23, 2017. He officially delayed implementation of the rule through another regulation[6] on July 11, 2017, six days before it was to go into effect.

There was an immediate uproar from the community that had fought so hard for the rule. And after successful litigation[7] lead by the National Venture Capital Association and others, USCIS was compelled [8] to accept cases in December 2017. By this time, however, many of my clients who wanted to apply under the IER, had fled to Canada. Some lawyers reported that about ten IER total cases were filed. One was eventually approved, though most remain pending to date.

In May 2018 the Trump administration issued the rule to rescind IER, but failed to complete the process. As a result, the rule remains on the books. The Biden administration can, in fact, revive the rule and implement it without delay.

While there's an opportunity now to also revise the rules to remove some of its more burdensome provisions, some of which I explain in the FAQ below, I am also aware that such a process will be time consuming for the new administration, especially when there are so many competing immigration priorities in a post-Trump era.

Therefore, I would suggest that the Biden administration revive this rule immediately with the intention to revise as soon as is practical. At least then we can allow these entrepreneurs to become part of the economic recovery solution. So, while Congress works on the Startup Visa as a permanent solution, the IER can save the day in the interim.

Update: On May 11th, just as I finalized the manuscript of this book, President Biden did, in fact, restore the International Entrepreneur Parole. We now have a path for international entrepreneurs to start their businesses in the US. It is a good stopgap while we continue to advocate for a Startup Visa to etch in the black and white letters of the law.

The following article was written January 16, 2017, on the blog of Watson Immigration Law. We are proud and honored that the Obama Administration used this article as part of its advocacy around the nation. The 'frequently asked question' section is printed here in its original format to preserve historic importance.

International Entrepreneurs Rule
FINAL RULE - JANUARY 2017
A Simplified Summary *by* Tahmina Watson

What kind of startup will qualify?

The key throughout the proposed rule is 'significant public benefit' and 'substantial potential for rapid growth and job creation.' These two defining phrases shape the rules.

The rules as drafted require the startup to show the following:

1. That it was created within the last 5 years of the application filing date. OR,
2. It was created within 5 years immediately before the receipt of grants, awards or investment.
3. Must be formed in the U.S. and operating lawfully in the U.S.
4. Must have substantial potential to experience rapid growth and job creation through significant attraction of capital investment or government grants and awards.
5. It excludes small businesses that are intended to generate income for the small business owners and their families.

How can I qualify as an entrepreneur?

USCIS will look for an entrepreneur who is 'well positioned to advance' his/her startup. The rules require the entrepreneur to prove 2 things:

1. That he/she owns a substantial interest in the startup, which has been defined as at least 10% of the entity at the time of application, and must maintain at least 5% throughout the parole period. And,
2. Has a central and active role in the operations of the startup.

What kind of investment in the startup will qualify?

There are two types of investments that will qualify:

1. Capital from U.S. investors with established records of successful investments.
2. Awards and grants from Federal, State or local governments.
3. An alternative criteria where one partially meets the above as long as one can provide compelling evidence of potential rapid growth.

Who is a Qualified U.S. investor and what are qualified investments?

1. A qualified U.S. investor can be a venture capitalist, angel investor or startup accelerator. If it's an individual, they must be a U.S. citizen or a green card holder. If an organization, it must be located in the U.S. and controlled by U.S. citizens.

2. The investment from a qualified investor must be at least $250,000.

3. The investor must have made similar investments over the last 5 years of no less than – $600,000. Additionally, at least 2 of the investment entities (startups) have generated at least $500,000 in revenue, with average annual growth of 20% OR at least 5 full-time jobs.

4. The investment must have been received within 18 months of filing the application.

5. The total sum can be a combination of investment made by one or more qualified investors.

6. Investment can be made in the form of 'other security convertible into equity commonly used in financing transactions.'

What kind of Grants or Awards will qualify?

1. A grant or an award for economic development from a federal, state or local government will qualify.

2. It cannot be a contract for goods or services that looks like an award/grant.

3. Minimum sum must be $100,000.

What if I don't raise the above amount of money, can I still qualify?

Yes. The rules provide alternative criteria for applicants who partially meet the above investments. If you do not meet the above requirement readily, you can show the following:

1. You have raised a substantial level of investment even if lower than the above amounts.

2. Provide 'reliable and compelling' evidence that the startup

will provide significant public benefit and has the substantial potential for rapid growth and job creation.

How do I apply?

1. A new form has been created for this particular application -
   - Form 941.
2. Filing fee is $1200.
3. An additional biometrics fee of $85 is required.
4. Must undertake biometrics -- meaning fingerprinting and a background check.
5. If in the U.S., you will attend a USCIS field office for biometrics. If outside the U.S., you will attend your local consulate.

Do I need to be earning an income already?

I'm afraid so. The U.S. wants to ensure that you do not become a public charge. As such, the rule proposes that the household income of an applicant is 400% above the Federal poverty guideline. That means, if a household income for a family of 3 is $20,020, then the entrepreneur will need to show a household income of $80,080.00.

However, this income can be combined with your spouse's annual income, too. These new provisions will allow your spouse to receive a work authorization.

What happens if my application is denied?

Unfortunately, you cannot appeal such a decision. It is important to remember that this is a discretionary provision and does not confer a right to a 'visa.' The rules do not state you cannot apply again though. The USCIS however can reopen a case on its own motion. Should the USCIS wish, the parole can also be revoked or terminated at any time.

Can my co-founders file too?

Yes. However, only up to 3 founders can apply from the same start-up. This is in line with the Invest Visa provisions from the comprehensive immigration reform bill 2013.

How long will I get to stay in the U.S. on this parole?

You will initially get 2.5 years. You can apply to renew the parole and will receive 2.5 more years. It is hoped that the business will be established enough that you (the founder(s)) can move on to a different immigrant or non-immigrant visa category (though, you may have to leave the U.S. to get the new visa).

What about my family?

Your spouse and children will be allowed to get parole too and live with you in the U.S. They will have to use the traditional application, form I-131, and also go through biometrics and background checks. Children under 14 don't have to pay the $85 biometrics fee though. The administration is mindful of family unity to ensure peace of mind.

What kind of work authorization will I get?

Thankfully, the administration has thought this out well. Work authorization will be incident to approval. That means you will get permission to work without having to apply for the traditional work authorization that can sometimes take up to 6 months to receive, the delay for which could hinder your startup. For I-9 purposes, the parole will be stamped to show work authorization and together with your passport, you will be able to satisfy that you have permission to work.

Your spouse will have to apply for work authorization in the traditional way though using form I-765 and pay the appropriate fees. No work authorization for children.

Do I have compliance issues to note?

Yes. The rules require that any change affecting the startup, referred to as 'material changes,' must be reported immediately. Material change could be a criminal charge, conviction, plea or any other criminal case or government administrative proceeding against the entrepreneur or the startup. Also, if at any time your ownership falls below 5%, your parole can be terminated or revoked.

Application to renew parole?

If you want to renew your parole, you must do the following:

1. File another Form I-941 within 90 days of expiration of current parole. Timing is important or else your parole will be terminated.
2. To qualify, your business must still be a startup and you must still be an entrepreneur as described above. You will have to prove the following:
3. You have received additional qualified investment during the parole period making the total investment $500,000. And-
4. Generated annual revenue of $500,000 with at least 20% average growth during the initial parole period. OR
5. Created at least – 5 full-time jobs for at least 35 hours a week, for employees that are U.S. citizens or green card holders.

What if I don't meet all the requirements for re-parole?

Fear not. The government has thought of this too. If you cannot meet the requirements fully, then you will have to show 'reliable and compelling' evidence that you have accomplished a substantial amount of the re-parole requirements mentioned above.

What happens while my re-parole is pending? Can I work?

Yes. Consistent with other non-immigrant visa categories, you will receive 240 days work permission while your re-parole application is pending.

Are there circumstances under which I could lose my parole?

Yes. Parole can be terminated at any time if it is thought your startup no longer serves a significant public benefit. This could be at any time, even without notice. There will be automatic termination at the end of the parole period or if your equity drops below 5%. If you receive a notice of intent to terminate, you will get 30 days to rebut any allegations.

If there is a violation that results in termination of parole of your spouse or child, you can still remain in the U.S., but the violator will not be able to remain.

This document was written in October 2016 in collaboration with the Washington Technology Industry Association and others. The comments for revision are important especially if we could revise the rules. The document is reprinted here in its original format to preserve historic importance.

October 17, 2016

Via Electronic Mail: uscisfrcomment@dhs.gov

Samantha Deshommes
Chief, Regulatory Coordination Division
Office of Policy and Strategy
U.S. Citizenship and Immigration Services
Department of Homeland Security
20 Massachusetts Avenue NW
Washington, DC 20529

Re: **International Entrepreneur Rule [CIS No. 2572-15; DHS Docket No. USCIS-2015-0006]**

Dear Ms. Deshommes,

Please find enclosed our comments on the proposed International Entrepreneur Rule. We appreciate the opportunity to review the rules and provide comments. Please do not hesitate to contact us if you have any questions.

Sincerely,

Michael Schutzler
CEO
Washington Technology Industry Association

Tahmina Watson
Founding Attorney
Watson Immigration Law

This document was written in October 2016 in collaboration with the Washington Technology Industry Association and others. The comments for revision are important especially if we could revise the rules. The document is reprinted here in its original format to preserve historic importance.

International Entrepreneurs Rule

PURPOSE OF COMMENTS: To improve the new proposed rule for international entrepreneurs as published in the Federal Register docket USCIS-2015-0006 by ensuring that said rule establishes and implements achievable requirements. We wish to facilitate successful application of the proposed rule in order to effectively create American jobs by immigrant entrepreneurs.

WHO WE ARE: We are leaders in the technology and entrepreneurship field in Seattle, Washington. We are venture capitalists, angel investors, startup accelerator investors/mentors, entrepreneurs, and professionals assisting people in the technology industry. Individually, each person has anywhere between 10 and 30 years of experience in their respective fields. Combined, we have over 100 years of experience. Our comments and suggestions are based on our experiences specifically working with rapid growth startups. Please find here a brief description of each group supporting these proposals:

Washington Technology Industry Association (WTIA) is the unifying voice in technology in Washington State. Our mission is to inform and motivate industry, education and government professionals; to collaborate productively in building education systems, physical infrastructure, and business climate; and ensure our region continues as one of the world's most influential technology hubs.

Watson Immigration Law is a boutique immigration law firm based in Seattle, Washington founded by Tahmina Watson. Our practice is primarily employment-based immigration law with an emphasis on startups and entrepreneurs. Tahmina Watson is the author of the book *The Startup Visa: Key to Job Growth and Economic Prosperity in America*.

Zoic Capital is a venture capital company that funds entrepreneurs and startups. We review over one thousand applications each year and select only the best for our portfolio. Our portfolio includes companies that have breakthrough technology and innovation that are changing the world. Our specialty lies in life sciences.

9 Miles Labs is one of the premier high-tech accelerators based in Seattle, Washington focused on enterprise, B2B software and cloud technologies.

Heather Redman, Angel Investor, is an experienced

investor who has been behind numerous successful companies. She is an accomplished lawyer, investor and community
leader. Among other things, Heather serves as a director of
the boards of WTIA and 9 Miles Labs.

SUMMARY:

Our work and experience demonstrate our passion for entrepreneurship and all that entrepreneurs offers. We especially recognize the
talent of immigrant entrepreneurs and the economic benefits they
bring to the United States. According to research from the Ewing
Marion Kauffman Foundation, startups create the most net jobs in
the United States.[9] Kauffman's research further confirms immigrants
are almost twice as likely to start businesses as native-born Americans. Research confirms 28.5 percent of new entrepreneurs in 2014
were immigrants, which is up from 13.3 percent in 1997 and about
one-quarter of the engineering and technology companies started in
the United States between 2006-2012 had at least one key founder
who was an immigrant.[10] Research also confirms that immigrant-
founded engineering and technology firms employed approximately
560,000 workers and generated $63 billion in sales in 2012. We can
say with confidence that some of these companies have been part of
our own portfolios.

We believe immigrant entrepreneurs are crucial for economic growth
and innovation. We have long felt the frustration that our immigration system does not include a path for entrepreneurs. Therefore, we
applaud the Administration for creating the International
Entrepreneur Rule. We support many of the provisions as reasonable
and implementable. In this document, we address the provisions that
we believe should be amended to ensure successful implementation
and workability of the rule in practice. We also would like to note

that many of our recommendations align with the provisions as drafted in the INVEST Visa provisions of S. 744 (113th) Border Security, Economic Opportunity, and Immigration Modernization Act (hereinafter referred to as S. 744).

RECOMMENDATIONS:

1. Formation of startup entity at time of initial application to be no more than 5 years.
2. Allow for revenue as consideration at the initial application stage.
3. Qualified investment amount should be reduced at the initial application stage.
4. Modify requirement of qualified investors.
5. Eliminate 'catch all' provision to allow applicant to apply or renew without meeting full requirements.
6. Reduce household income to 125% and allow savings as an alternative option.
7. Allow initial parole period to be 3 years.
8. Allow equity of applicant to fall below 10%.
9. Re-parole requirements of revenue generation and job creation.
10. Recognize 'bootstrapping' and provide guidance.
11. Guidance for those entrepreneurs who 'exit' during the parole period.
12. Reduce filing fees from $1200, allow Premium Processing, and suggested filing and adjudication procedures.

DETAILED COMMENTS:

1. Formation of startup entity at the time of initial application to be no more than 5 years.

- The initial stage of a startup is experimental. It takes significant time to develop the startup to a stage where it can seek funding. To require that the entity is no more than 3 years old will exclude many entities that required time to obtain funding. Often 3 years is not enough time to have raised the requisite funding amount necessary to be eligible for these rules.
- In practice, a startup can only be productive after the first round of funds is received. Some companies call themselves startups up until IPO, examples of which include companies like Apptio, Inc.

We suggest that the startup must be formed no more than 5 years from the time of application.

2. Allow revenue as an alternative requirement for initial eligibility.

- Some startup entities are successful from the outset. Such entities often will have generated significant revenue and American jobs. Such entities may not have needed to raise funds from qualified investors, or if they had, they did not need much funding. The bootstrapping model (which we address below) is an example of revenue growth before raising funds.
- In past startup visa bills introduced in Congress over the last 6 years, revenue was a consistent eligibility option. S.744

allowed eligibility of $250,000 revenue in the last 2 years and the creation of 3 qualified jobs.

We propose that a similar requirement be allowed so that those entrepreneurs who have proven themselves by generating revenue and jobs are afforded the opportunity to apply for parole with a combination of revenue and job creation already accomplished.

Therefore, we suggest that the requirement be aligned with S.744 as $250,000 and 3 qualified jobs in the last 2 years.

3. Qualified investment amount should be reduced at the initial application stage.

- While the range of investment can vary significantly, most technology companies will raise $250,000 on average.
- $250,000 was the amount listed in the very first Startup Visa Act 2010 S. 3029.
- S.744 outlined measures for a non-immigrant X-visa. The X-visa required $100,000 as an initial investment. Past bills had proposed requirements that were more aligned with general practice.
- WTIA conducted research specifically for submission with these comments.[11] The research was based on WTIA's database of funding information. It found that of 116 tech companies founded in 2013, 98 of them received funding within 3 years and the average deal size across the 116 companies was $2.1 million. Of the 116 companies, 18 did not receive any funding at all. If we were to go with the International Entrepreneur Rule the way it's currently written, only 56% of the businesses got at least $350k in funding within 3 years and **this includes all founders,**

both foreign- and American-born. Of the 860 tech companies founded between 2010-2016, 487 received funding, 127 received no funding, and 246 didn't have any deal data. This means the average deal size across all companies was $3.89 million. This includes companies that may have received funding in the 6th year. The research shows that it can take more than 3 years to receive funding for some technology companies.

- In addition, foreign-born founders generally have more difficulty in obtaining funding. This is because they have less access to and connection to angels and venture capitalists.

Reducing the initial funding requirement will be more practical for immigrant entrepreneurs. We therefore recommend the initial funding threshold be reduced to $250,000.

4. Modify requirement of qualified investors.

- The proposed rules as drafted define qualified investors as venture capital firms, angel investors, and startup-accelerators. Organizations must be controlled by U.S. citizens or legal permanent residents (LPRs). Angel investors must be U.S. citizens or LPRs. The requirements further qualify this category by requiring the investor to have made similar investments in the last 5 years and that at least 2 of the investments have generated at least $500,000 or 5 full time jobs.

We request you to remove this condition of revenue/job creation.

- Most qualified investors as defined in these rules will have made previous investments. Most investors will likely also be able to demonstrate past revenue/job creation. But many abled and experienced investors may believe that the burden is too high. While we appreciate the reason for setting such stringent restrictions is to prevent fraudulent investments, it will be an unnecessarily difficult condition. For example, it is standard practice in non-immigrant temporary work visa applications such as H-1B or L-1s for USCIS to request payroll taxes, W-2s, W-3s, etc. In EB-5 petitions, one must prove job creation with similar documents including form I-9s. To implement this, the qualified investor will have to obtain documents from an unrelated entity and share documents that are otherwise confidential. The practical impact will be burdensome not only to the investor but also to the unrelated third parties. As such, it could prevent investors from participating.

Therefore, we suggest that the additional alternative requirement of past revenue generation and job creation for similar startups is removed because it will prevent the successful use of the rule.

5. Eliminate 'catch all' provision to allow applicant to apply or renew without meeting full requirements.

- Entrepreneurs who do not successfully meet the requirements should not be allowed re-parole. If a startup has not met the above requirements, it may be an indication that the startup does not have the potential of rapid growth. It may lead to affording opportunities to undeserving candidates who may not have the potential of significant public benefit.
- The combination of lowering the initial investment amount

and lengthening the parole period to 3 years will enable the right applicants to prove themselves.

Based on the above information, we suggest this provision be eliminated as long the initial parole period is extended to 3 years.

6. Reduce household income to 125% and allow savings as an alternative option.

Income:

- Entrepreneurs are known to live frugally and will save every penny for their startups. They will house-share, live with parents, and find ways to live beneath their means. In addition, for maximum success of the startup, founders will often pay their employees or make business expenses before taking a salary.
- As such, requiring 400% above the poverty guideline is unreasonable and will prevent almost all international entrepreneurs from utilizing the parole.

Instead, we suggest aligning this requirement to be consistent with other areas of immigration law. For example, we were happy to see that the proposed rule allows for 240 days of work authorization during the pending period of the re-parole application. Earlier this year, through executive action, your agency brought this consistency to all non-immigrant work visas, such as E-3 and H-1B1 applications. Using the same idea to keep rules consistent where they can be, the household income rules should be consistent with current family-based immigration law.

- Family-based immigration law requires a sponsor of a

relative to demonstrate a household income of $125% above the poverty guidelines.[12]

Therefore, we also suggest that the entrepreneur be allowed to show a household income of 125% above the poverty guideline.

Savings:

- In addition, in keeping with family-based immigration law, allow applicants to show savings as an alternative option. We suggest that, aligned with the income requirement, one year's salary at 125% of the Federal Poverty Guideline is shown in savings as an alternative.
- The Canadian Startup Visa was based on the first bill presented in U.S. Congress in 2010.[13] The Canadian Startup Visa has been in effect since in April 2013 and has seen much success. It requires the entrepreneur to have savings referred to as 'settlement funds'[14] which appear to be based on a similar poverty guideline. There is no household income requirement in the Canadian visa requirement. We suggest that this model be used as an alternative requirement. The below is what the Canadian website states regarding settlement funds:

Bring sufficient settlement funds

The Government of Canada does not provide financial support to new Start-up Visa immigrants. You must show that you have enough money to support yourself and your dependents after you arrive in Canada. You cannot borrow this money from another person. You will need to provide proof that you have the money when you submit your application. The amount you will need depends on the size of your family. These amounts are updated every year.

How much money should you bring?
Find out how much it costs to live where you are planning to
settle in Canada.

Applicant's spouse's income:
We applaud that the entrepreneur's spouse will be given
work authorization and that the spouse's income will be
considered as part of the household income. However, it is
unclear from the proposed rules, whether the spouse's
income in the foreign country will be taken into account.
Please clarify.

*We suggest that foreign income can be relied upon to meet the house-
hold income threshold.*

7. Allow initial parole period to be 3 years.

- An average startup needs approximately 3 years to achieve
  the measures listed in these rules to qualify for parole. As
  such, 2 years is insufficient time.
- In addition, most other employment-based non-immigrant
  work visas allow a maximum 3-year period of approval.

*To bring consistency with other areas of temporary work visas, and to
provide sufficient time to demonstrate success, allow the initial period
of the parole to be 3 years.*

8. Allow equity of applicant to fall below 10%.

- Prominent entrepreneur Peter Thiel teaches the following:

Building a valuable company is a long journey. A key question to keep your eye on as a founder is dilution. The Google founders had 15.6% of the company at IPO. Steve Jobs had 13.5% of Apple when it went public in the early '80s. Mark Pincus had 16% of Zynga at IPO. If you have north of 10% after many rounds of financing, that's generally a very good outcome. Dilution is relentless.[15]

- It is vitally important to know how many shares the entrepreneur held during the initial parole. However, upon accepting further investments, those shares would be diluted and can fall below 10%. Holding this standard could render the parole rules ineffective.

- More than 80% of the startups in the Seattle area founded by immigrants were founded by teams, not individuals. Therefore, a 10% equity stake could be a fair and relevant standard if applied to the founding team. Consider the case where 10% as an individual stake would be reasonable on the day of formation with a team of four founders, where each owns 25%. However, after a seed round which is typically 30% dilution and an A round which is typically 45% dilution including the ESOP required by almost every Venture Capitalist, those same 4 founders would already be below the 10% equity rule despite great success in raising money and creating jobs. On the other hand, the 4 founders together still would own north of 36% of the company.

We suggest that this requirement is removed or reduced significantly.

9. Re-parole requirements of revenue generation and job creation.

- We support the funding/revenue/employment numbers in these rules for re-parole. They are reasonable **in the tech industry so long as the initial parole period is 3 years.**

We support the re-parole requirements, given that the initial parole period be 3 years.

10. Recognize 'bootstrapping' and provide guidance.

- Bootstrapping is a common way to create a startup. In this model, the founder starts with savings or funds from friends and family. It then acquires customers and generates revenue. In due course, as the business expands, it seeks funding.[16] Seattle is specifically known for its bootstrapping startups. Many such startups are successful and would be considered rapid growth companies. A recent modern example of such a company is Dry Bar. Dry Bar, based in California, is not a technology company but a hair salon providing hair drying services only. It currently employs 1000 stylists in 43 locations.[17] Other successful bootstrap enterprises include Facebook, Microsoft, Dell, etc.
- Bootstrapping companies may be able to raise sufficient revenue and thus may meet the requirements of these proposed rules. This is another reason to allow revenue generation as an alternative requirement for eligibility.

Given that bootstrapping is a different but successful model for rapid growth companies, recognition and guidance of such a model must be included in these rules.

. . .

11. Guidance for those entrepreneurs who 'exit' during the parole period.

- The ultimate goal for founders and qualified investors is to exit the startup. Exits can be in the form of IPOs or acquisitions. The average timeframe for an IPO is about 7 years from first financing.[18] The average exit can take anywhere between 4 to 8.6 years.[19]
- Should the startup entity be 3 (or 5 years as we suggest) years at the time of filing for parole, it is not inconceivable that there could be an exit during the parole or re-parole period.

We suggest that guidance and options are provided for such entrepreneurs who clearly will have contributed to the significant public benefit of the United States and should not be subject to immediate termination of parole.

12. Lower filing fees from $1200, allow Premium Processing, and suggested filing and adjudication procedures.

Filing fees:

- While we appreciate that entrepreneurs will be given an opportunity to file for parole and work on their startups, a $1200 filing fee is high. Other employment-based visa application fees based on Form I-129 are significantly lower at $325 with additional supplemental fees depending on visa type. For example, an L-1 visa application fee including the requisite supplemental fee is $825 ($325 + $500 fraud fee); an H-1B fee is $1525 ($325+500+750); an O-1 is $325.

Parole is not a visa and will not confer any status. The fee should reflect the admission benefit and not be high simply because a new benefit is being created. We suggest that the fee is reduced.

Premium Processing:

- In addition, we suggest that Premium Processing is allowed in these cases. Startups often will lose opportunities without swift action. Also, startup founders will not be able to work on their startups if they are already in the U.S. on a different non-immigrant visa. As such, Premium Processing will allow quick transition into working for the startup and thus working towards rapid growth and significant public benefit.

USCIS Entrepreneur in Residence Team:

- We also take the opportunity to request that these applications are adjudicated by the USCIS Entrepreneur in Residence team. In 2012, when the USCIS EIR team was instituted, immigration officers were trained specifically on entrepreneurship issues. That training and understanding is reflected in their adjudication and will be invaluable in adjudicating international entrepreneur parole application.

Creation of a 'Known Qualified Investor' Program:

- Investors will often invest in same or similar companies and will likely have a series of investments in different immigrant founded companies. We believe it will be efficient for USCIS, as well as the investor, to create a 'known qualified investor' program, similar to the 'Known Employer Pilot' program recently created by USCIS.[20] Under the Known Employer Pilot, employers will file an application to request that USCIS predetermine certain requirements of select immigrant and non-immigrant visa classifications that relate to the employer itself. These requirements generally relate to the employer's corporate structure, operations, and financial health. This pilot process means that in adjudicating an individual petition or application, a USCIS officer will not need to review those approved employer eligibility requirements unless the facts have changed since USCIS made its predetermination or there are indications of fraud or material misrepresentation. Instead, the officer will only have to decide on the remaining requirements of an individual petition or application, such as the nature of the job offered and the employee's qualifications.[21]

We suggest that a similar program for qualified investors will assist the overall adjudication process and believe that creating such a program at the outset of implementation of the rule will be helpful in the long run.

CONCLUSION:

We applaud the Administration for introducing the proposed rule for international entrepreneurs; it will fill a significant void in our current immigration system. However, we believe that our above comments and suggestions would make the proposed rule more effective.

Should you wish to contact any of us, we would be happy to provide more information.

We thank you in advance for the efforts in preparing such complicated new policy.

Supporters

Group	Contact Name	Website	Location
Washington Technology Industry Association	Michael Schutlzer CEO	www.washingtontechnology.org	Seattle, Washington
Watson Immigration Law	Tahmina Watson Immigration Attorney	www.watsonimmigrationlaw.com	Seattle, Washington
Zoic Capital	Neal Mody Managing Partner	www.zoiccapital.com	Seattle, Washington
Heather Redman	Heather Redman Angel Investor	www.linkedin.com/in/hredman	Seattle, Washington
9 Miles Lab	Sanjay Puri Co-founder	www.9milelabs.com	Seattle, Washington

7

CHANGES WITHOUT CONGRESS
PART II
OTHER EXECUTIVE ACTIONS

The President of the United States and his administration has the authority to make administrative, regulatory and policy changes without Congressional input. As such, the Biden administration can make significant improvements to other immigration policies, in addition to the International Entrepreneur Rule discussed in the previous chapter, through executive action. And while the new administration likely has some strategies in the works, I have some ideas, based on more than a decade of working on this issue.

Before I dive into my suggestions for change, however, I would first suggest that they review President Obama's November 2014,[1] memorandum titled "Modernizing and Streamlining the U.S. Immigrant Visa System for the 21st Century." After issuing the memo, the Obama administration published a notice on the Federal Register to request public comments.[2] The notice stated that the administration was "directing the Secretaries of State and Homeland Security, in consultation with other cabinet secretaries and the White House, to make recommendations to streamline and improve the nation's legal immigration system. Such efforts should focus on reducing Government costs, improving services for applicants, reducing burdens on employers, and combating waste, fraud, and abuse in the system, while safeguarding the interests of American workers." (DHS Docket No. USCIS-2014-0014, Document No. 2014-30641).

The notice garnered much attention at the time. While I personally spent a significant amount of time drafting comments (reprinted at the back of this book), I know that many of my colleagues, organizations and individuals spent an equal amount of time providing comments and suggestions to improve the immigration system. Those comments are invaluable. The Biden administration should dust them off and review them in their entirety for inspiration and creative action. While the landscape changed significantly between 2017 and 2021, those comments came directly from the public on a multitude of issues that we are still grappling with today.

Founder friendly administrative, regulatory and policy amendments

Current visa options and related regulations should be reviewed to make them more entrepreneur friendly. Here are some suggestions:

Expand premium processing for certain immigrant visa applications

In the first edition of this book, I mentioned that President Obama would take action on the National Interest Waiver (NIW), an immigrant visa category, commonly referred to as EB2. This waiver is an exemption by which "exceptional" foreign nationals can bypass the burdensome labor certification process to obtain a green card if they can prove their presence here "is in the interest of the United States."[3]

As discussed in Chapter 3, the requirements for this visa category were difficult for entrepreneurs to meet until a precedent-setting case was handed down from the Administrative Appeals Office in December 2016. *Matter of Dhanasar*[4] created a new and more reasonable framework to demonstrate the national interest of an applicant and their work. As a result, obtaining green cards under this category became somewhat easier for immigrant entrepreneurs.

However, processing time for such cases can be long. Even before Covid-19 slowed most immigration case processing to a snail's pace, we could expect 9 to 12 months for NIW cases. At the time of this writing, we remain in the grip of the pandemic and the backlog continues.

In September 2020, Congress passed a bill titled "Emergency Stopgap USCIS Stabilization Act,"[5] expanding premium processing to several visa categories. The act specifically allowed USCIS to accept additional fees to process NIW cases within 15 calendar days. It is currently available in a handful of situations. However, the provision has not been implemented. Congress has created the path and USCIS has authority to implement it. There is no time like the present.

In Chapter 3, we discussed the L-1A visa. There is a similar immigrant visa for these types of cases, and that is known as the multinational transfer visa for managers or executives. It is commonly known as EB1(C), and allows executives or managers transferring from a foreign branch of a U.S. company to apply for green cards. Often such executives are founders or shareholders of the company abroad and are in the United States on an L-1A visa. After one year of continuous business operations, the entity can apply for a green card for the executive or founder. However, while there is premium processing available for an L-1A application, it is not available for the EB1(C) application.

Similar to the NIW situation above, such cases are also taking a long time to process. But ordinarily, these cases can take 8-10 months to process. There are many reasons for a founder to have immigration security. Raising further rounds of funding, or expanding office locations beyond the one mentioned in the application form, are a few examples. Implementing premium processing for such cases is good for business reasons not just for the founder, but also for the U.S. economy.

Concurrent filing of Form I-485

Another problem we expected would be addressed through executive action at the time we published the first edition of this book, was the timing of when a green card application, or Form I-485, can be filed for those here on certain temporary, employment-based visas, such as H-1B and L-1. Such applications have various stages of intensely tedious steps to follow. Filing for adjustment of status, as it is called, is the final one.

Currently, Form I-485 can only be filed once the person reaches the front of the line.[6] This so-called line, or the length of time one has to wait for a green card to become available for them, is often in excess of 11 years for citizens of countries such as India and China[7].

President Biden could establish a process to allow green card applications, or Form I-485s, to be filed earlier in this lengthy, exhaustive timeline, so that applicants can receive work authorization sooner than they do now. By filing the form, one is eligible to obtain a work authorization document. Work authorization in this context gives these workers flexibility to move from one employer to another, which is often crucial for career advancement and development. It will also give them the freedom to travel abroad more easily. The actual green card will be issued only when the person reaches the front of the line.

Why does this concern entrepreneurs? Currently, when work-visa holders reach the point where they can apply for green cards, they can use their aforementioned work authorization to gain self-employment. This policy change alone will have a direct benefit to the U.S. economy, while allowing immigrants to start their own companies sooner.

Allow for flexibility in entrepreneur job descriptions and employer control

Firstly, stop applying the Neufeld Memo[8] to founders. The memo, developed in 2010 in response to fraud investigations, provides guidelines which require employers of H-1B visa holders to demonstrate an employer-employee relationship. Evidence of such relationships include providing IRS Form W4, employment contracts, job descriptions, and more to the USCIS. In essence, USCIS assesses whether the employer will maintain complete control over the person's employment. And while entrepreneurs can apply for an H-1B through their own businesses, they must prove the business controls their employment. This is done by demonstrating that another shareholder or the board of directors have the authority to hire, fire or supervise the entrepreneur's work. In practice, this 'control' often stumps the entrepreneurial spirit, the vision and action of the entrepreneur. As a result, the business can fail.

Additionally, H-1B visas require a job description that is based on the entrepreneur's educational background and the position they will hold. In other words, there needs to be a nexus between the academic and theoretical training of someone with a Bachelor's degree, to the job they will hold. For example, a doctor would not be approved to work as an architect. These distinctions can become tricky in technology related jobs. Such as, is a computer science degree sufficient for a position as a data analyst?

Furthermore, these job descriptions must be focused on the position itself. However, an entrepreneur who needs to focus on operating their businesses will often have many roles in addition to those described under the terms of their H-1B visas. For example, as a business owner, I am not only a lawyer, but also a human resources manager, marketing manager, bookkeeper, and supervisor and perform countless other roles. Therefore, there needs to be some specific policies in place for entrepreneurs as the lack of flexibility and autonomy will impede their success.

Allow non-cash compensation as part of a founder's salary

Secondly, we should allow the use of cash substitutes, such as stock valuation, convertible notes, and other regularly used compensation methods instead of cash-only wages for founders. This is especially important when an H1-B candidate is launching the startup and where the regulations require a minimum salary. Startups generally cannot afford high wages, particularly in the early stages. They get their companies to the point where they can be evaluated for funding by investors. I understand the policy argument against cash substitutes might be fear of the entrepreneur, becoming a public charge. But the USCIS could institute procedures to monitor and police that, revoking the visa of anyone who resorts to public assistance. This should also apply to other visa categories for which startup founders might be eligible.

Greater consideration to non-cash investments and assets

Thirdly, modify current policies in various other visa categories to enable startup founders to obtain visas. For example, with some reinterpretation and policy changes, options such as the E-2 investor visa, TN, the North American Free Trade Agreement visa, and O-1, the visa for those with extraordinary ability, can be used for founders more effectively. For the E-2 treaty visa, for example, I suggest the investment also include the value of intellectual property and other intangible assets, since startup founders do not often have a lot of money but have rich minds and valuable intellectual property.

Clear guidance on ownership interest for TN visa holders

While TN visa holders are generally not allowed to be self-employed, the written law does not prevent some ownership. The Foreign Affairs Manual states at 9 FAM 402.17-5(A)(3), that a foreign national cannot qualify for a TN visa to establish a business or practice in the United States in which the professional will be, in substance, self-employed. In other words, an entrepreneur who does not have controlling shares and who is employed by the startup, should qualify for a TN visa. This is often the case when there are several co-founders and none have controlling shares.

There needs to be guidance from the Department of Homeland Security (DHS) to all its agencies so that adjudication across the board is consistent. Many Canadians could actually come to the U.S. and start their companies if minority ownership interests are not treated as a death knell to the TN application.

. . .

Remove requirements for physical office space

Additionally, we should allow the USCIS to recognize modern business practices which include the use of home offices, virtual offices and incubators as legitimate work places -- particularly in the H-1B and L-1 context. In the world of modern technology, one only needs a laptop, a printer and phone to conduct a successful business.

There are many examples of successful businesses that started without office space. For example, Facebook got its start in a university dorm room. Yet the USCIS typically views home offices or virtual offices with suspicion. Random site visits investigating fraudulent cases are common in H-1B and L-1 cases.

Interestingly enough, because of the Covid-19 pandemic, regulations were updated for E-2 investor visas in July 2020,[9] removing requirements for formal office space. Since the 2020 global pandemic began, many businesses in the U.S. have struggled to stay afloat. At the time of writing this book, the pandemic continues in earnest and many businesses have closed. The U.S. Department of State's Foreign Affairs Manual (FAM) at section 9 FAM 402.9-4(D) states, "An applicant does not necessarily need a physical office space to qualify for an E visa. Although having physical office space may be relevant in determining whether the requirements for an E visa have been met, it is not a requirement to qualify for the visa."

If we had to take away only one lesson from the global pandemic, it is that people can and do work from home successfully. With modern technology, multimillion-dollar businesses are operating without physical office space. While this has been recognized in the E-2 context, only because of the pandemic, the flexibility could and should now be extended to cover the H-1B, L-1 and other visa categories, especially for startups.

The way we do business has evolved, and if anything, evolved exponentially due to the Covid-19 pandemic. Our policies, therefore, must change as well.

Encourage universities to be engaged in the immigrant entrepreneur journey

What else can be done without Congress? We can use more flexibility within existing laws. For example, H-1B visa holders employed at universities in the U.S. are not subject to the annual H-1B cap. That means universities can hire promising and talented graduates in appropriate roles, while those graduates work simultaneously on their startups until they reach the point where they can qualify for self-employment.[10] The Global Entrepreneur in Residence (GEIR) coalition actually formalized this as a program that has been implemented in several universities around the country. As Brad Feld mentions in his foreword to this book, the program has been wildly successful in creating jobs and financial contributions to our economy. The administration can encourage universities around the country to be more engaged and adopt this program. It is a win-win for the university, for the immigrant entrepreneur and for the country.

Revive the USCIS Entrepreneur in Residence Program

In his second term, before leaving office, President Obama took several steps to address immigration policy as it relates to entrepreneurs. Under the leadership of the then-director of USCIS and now Secretary of DHS, Alejandro Mayorkas, the Entrepreneur in Residence program (EIR) was created in 2012. The program trained a team of immigration officers on cutting edge entrepreneurial issues to work with startup firms, recognizing these firms and their founders have specific concerns that need careful consideration by experts.

Incubators and shared work-spaces gained credibility through this program. It made a very real and positive impact on case adjudication. I was honored to participate in the launch event that was held in Silicon Valley, California in 2012 and observed first-hand the laudable efforts to create this program.

The administration went further and created an Entrepreneur Portal on the USCIS website. It essentially consisted of a visa guide of simple questions to enable applicants to assess what visa category would be best for them. It was a welcome update. However, the Trump administration removed the portal soon after taking office. My suggestion would be that the Biden administration revive this program as a priority.

Conclusion

Immigration officers can only work within the parameters of policies that exist. It is these policies that need to be adjusted to match modern business practices. The Trump administration was successful in limiting immigration, dismantling the immigration system, and creating obstacles in all types of immigration cases by executive action, regulatory changes and policy memos. He didn't have Congress to help with his goals. President Biden can make significant changes to better the immigration system in the same way. I believe the above suggestions I make will have a positive impact, not just for immigrant entrepreneurs but for the entire immigration system, to benefit America.

CONCLUSION

From pre-revolution Jamestown Settlement to present-day Silicon Valley, immigrants have had a hand in invention and innovation. From laying down railroad tracks to cutting-edge technology, they've helped to modernize the U.S. in every era.

Today, however, we are at an impasse in our immigration system that is blocking the next generation of inventors, innovators and entrepreneurs from bringing their ideas to the U.S. and preventing the ones already here as students or temporary workers from staying.

The idea of driver-less cars and the bionic eye are now within our grasp. But the potential for further, awe-inspiring advancements is beyond even our comprehension or imagination. As Vivek Wadhwa describes in a recent article, moon travel will be within reach for the everyday traveler, thanks to entrepreneurs.[1]

But not all those entrepreneurs are in the U.S. Innovative ideas are alive in the minds of people from countries all across the globe – from Mexico to Singapore, Pakistan to Romania to Canada.

Think of a country like India. What were once the slums of Bombay, are now producing some of today's boldest innovators. Countries like India are becoming technology hubs, with U.S.-educated Indian nationals returning home in droves to create new businesses, because of our restrictive immigration policies. But not just in India.

There was a time when technology was so costly, it was out of reach and off limits to the majority of Americans. And in distant parts of the world, people could only dream of linking to the internet. But today, travel to any country, even some of the most remote parts of distant nations, and you see people walking about with cell phones – often smart phones – in hand, or sitting in coffee shops or public parks using tablets and laptops. Such accessibility has also made it easier for entrepreneurs to generate and implement their ideas, which in turn has become the basis for startup firms. In some cases, they need little more than a computer and a telephone.

The truth is entrepreneurship can happen and is happening everywhere – on scales both small and large. To capture the vitality and economic growth foreign entrepreneurs and startups can bring, other countries rising out of the ashes of the last global financial crisis, are offering them a welcome embrace.[2] Yet, America remains a silent bystander in this global competition. Today, the Chinese e-commerce company, Alibaba, is nipping at Amazon's heels. Tomorrow, who knows?

While this book has focused on the technology industry, the Startup Visa will apply to other sectors, too. Entrepreneurs and small business owners – from Main Street to Wall Street – are the backbone of the U.S. economy. Nevertheless, it is the technology revolution and global competition that are fueling this urgent need.

As Eric Lui, senior law lecturer at University of Washington and CEO of Citizen University, which works to help Americans build a culture of citizenship, stated, "The U.S. is an incubator for the world where ideas are spread around the planet."[3] For the U.S. to continue to spread ideas, to remain globally competitive, to bring talent to our shores, our immigration laws must change.

In a constantly evolving and ever-shrinking global economy, creation of the Startup Visa should not even be in question.

CORRESPONDENCE WITH PRESIDENT OBAMA AND FORMER NEW YORK MAYOR AND PRESIDENTIAL CANDIDATE MICHAEL BLOOMBERG

I had so much hope for comprehensive immigration reform in 2013. But when it was clear that we lost the opportunity for immigration reform, I wrote to President Obama urging him to take executive action on immigration issues. I was very grateful to receive a response from him. Here is a copy of my letter and his reply.

1001 4th Avenue, Suite 3200
Seattle, WA, 98154
Tel: (206) 292-5237
Fax: (866) 669-6822
Cell: (206) 856-3808
http://www.watsonimmigrationlaw.com
Email: tahmina@watsonimmigrationlaw.com

Principal: Tahmina Watson, admitted NY State

April 17, 2014

Via Office of Senator Patty Murray
President Barak Obama
White House
1600 Pennsylvania Avenue NW
Washington, DC 20500

Dear Mr. President,

My name is Tahmina Watson. I am an immigration attorney in Seattle, Washington. I emigrated from London, England in 2005 when I married my husband, Thomas Watson, a patent attorney at Amin, Turocy and Watson. I became a US citizen in 2011 after the birth of my first daughter Sofia, 4 years old now. My second daughter Sarina is 21 months old.

As an immigrant myself, I believe it is a privilege to help others' dreams come true, whether they are employers finding talented employees, business owners opening new companies or family-members being reunited. Yet I have found that, for entrepreneurs, our current immigration law is falling far short of its potential.

In 2009, when I founded Watson Immigration Law, I immediately saw a recurring problem of people stuck in the green card backlog, but wanting to start their own companies. However, the lack of a suitable visa prevented these talented individuals from doing so. Soon thereafter, the first Startup Visa Act was introduced in Congress and it was then that I became more passionate than ever about the subject.

Over the next few years, I followed the path of the Startup Visa Act closely. When the Senate immigration bill S.744 dropped in April 2013, I lost sleep for several weeks studying the Startup visa provisions in detail. It led to the distinct privilege of assisting Senator Moran's office draft amendments to those provisions.

As a practitioner, my views are different from those who deal with policy alone. As a business owner, I understand the Startup visa. As an immigrant entrepreneur, I know about the hard work entrepreneurs devote to creating successful businesses. This new visa category is key to retaining talent, creating jobs and growing the US economy. While the new economy pulled us out of the last recession, without the Startup visa, we will curb important economic growth and lose the best and the brightest to countries who understand their importance. I would welcome the opportunity to assist, advocate and advise in bringing change to this area of the law.

The Senate bill S.744 and House bill HR15 provide a sound foundation for an entrepreneur visa. The provisions in the House SKILLs visa Act H.R. 2131, as they stand, are unreasonable, and will lead to a Startup Visa in name only.

With sincere hopes of immigration reform this year, I wanted to stop nothing short of trying to make my voice be heard by you directly. The United States needs a Startup Visa so we continue to the lead the world in innovation and job growth.

I recognize the immensely difficult task you face and give thanks for your hard work and determination in fighting for immigration reform. I also commend you for your administration's Startup America initiative and USCIS's Entrepreneur in Residence program. Still, more needs to be done. I urge you to use your executive powers until Congress cooperates.

Thank you for reading my letter. I will look forward to hearing from you.

Sincerely,

Tahmina Watson

August 28, 2014

Ms. Tahmina Watson
Seattle, Washington

Dear Tahmina:

Thank you for writing. I appreciate hearing from you.

Our Nation faces serious challenges, and we will only overcome them by involving all Americans in shaping the policies that affect their own lives. My Administration is continuously working to engage individuals in innovative ways. I encourage you to explore www.WhiteHouse.gov, which is regularly updated and more interactive than ever before.

Thank you, again, for contacting me and providing your thoughtful suggestions.

Sincerely,

Ms. Tahmina Watson
1001 Fourth Avenue
Seattle, Washington 98154

MICHAEL R. BLOOMBERG

April 23, 2015

Ms. Tahmina Watson
Watson Immigration Law
1001 4th Avenue, Suite 3200
Seattle, WA 98154

Dear Ms. Watson:

Thank you for sending me a copy of *The Startup Visa*. Immigration reform is key to ensuring the future economic prosperity of our nation, and I appreciate your dedication to this critical issue.

Many thanks for sharing your work with me, and congratulations on this great achievement.

All the best.

Sincerely,

Michael R. Bloomberg

MRB:jr

TAHMINA TALKS
IMMIGRATION – PODCAST

Tahmina is the host of the popular podcast *Tahmina Talks Immigration*.

Inspired by this book release, she created The Startup Visa series. Nationally renowned thought leaders on the issue, as well as international leaders on entrepreneurship share their thoughts on why such a visa category is essential in the United States. Most of the episodes were recorded before the International Entrepreneur Program was restored by the Biden administration.

In any event, please do subscribe to the podcast and to our social media accounts to ensure you hear updates on the book release and episode updates.

Thank you to each and every one of the guests listed on the following pages for appearing in the series and for their tireless work for over a decade trying to establish a Startup Visa right here in the United States.

Tahmina Talks Immigration®

Startup Visa Series

STUART ANDERSON
Executive Director, National Foundation for American Policy

JOHN DEARIE
Founder and President, Center for American Entrepeneurship

JEFF FARRAH
General Counsel, National Venture Capital Association

BRAD FELD
Foundry Group Partner, Techstars Co-Founder

CRAIG MONTOURI
Co-Founder and Executive Director, Global Entrepreneur in Residence Coalition

VALENTINA PRIMO
Founder, Startups Without Borders

https://tahminatalksimmigration.buzzsprout.com

 Listen on **Apple Podcasts**   **Spotify**    **YouTube**

Tahmina Talks Immigration®

Startup Visa Series

NINA ROBERTS
US Journalist and Photographer, The Xeno Files Project

MICHAEL SCHUTZLER
CEO, Washington Technology Industry Association

DANISH SOOMRO
Founder, visadb.io

TROY VOSSELLOR
Co-Founder, gener8or

JASON WIENS
Policy Director, Kauffman Foundation

https://tahminatalksimmigration.buzzsprout.com

 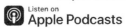 

ABOUT TAHMINA WATSON
AN EFFECTIVE, PROLIFIC CHAMPION IN
IMMIGRATION LAW

Tahmina Watson, the founder in 2009 of Watson Immigration Law, has distinguished herself as a successful and committed specialist in United States immigration law. She has helped hundreds of businesses and families achieve their goals for working and living in the United States.

Nationally recognized in this complex arena of law, Tahmina is herself a U.S. immigrant (and naturalized citizen), having moved to the United States in 2005 from her birthplace in London, U.K., where she received her education and initial training in law. As a result, she possesses an understanding and empathy that make her work as much a calling as a career.

Tahmina represents U.S. and multinational companies that need high-skilled workers from other countries, non-U.S. businesses opening offices in this country, start-ups with founders from other countries, and investors expanding their businesses in the U.S.

Her work with noncitizen founders and co-founders led to her national advocacy for a startup visa, working with Obama era White House officials on visa options for startup founders, advocating in the media and to writing this book.

Her work in family immigration has succeeded in uniting many spouses, parents and children so that they can enjoy stable, cohesive family units.

A broad public profile

Tahmina is a member of the bar in New York State and Washington State. She was a practicing barrister in the United Kingdom before immigrating, and is currently an unregistered barrister in England and Wales.

She is a well-known media figure in the immigration field. In the Seattle area, where she and her family live, Tahmina is the host of the popular radio show turned podcast "Tahmina Talks Immigration®". She has contributed opinion pieces to numerous publications, including The Washington Examiner, Seattle Times, *YES! Magazine, Huffington Post,* and *Entrepreneur*. Tahmina is a Leadership Network Contributor to *Entrepreneur*. She is also a columnist with the distinguished legal publication *Above the Law*.

Nationally, Forbes, Bloomberg and CNN are among the news outlets that frequently tap her for her expertise. Her blog, Watson Immigration Law, reaches a wide audience.

Volunteerism: a driving force

Tahmina's volunteer work has always been integral to her professional life. She points to the work she did as an undergraduate, helping children with special needs as the spark that later led to offering her knowledge of the law to their parents, as they sought educational opportunities for their children.

She led a human rights group in law school and has volunteered with numerous nonprofits since coming to the U.S.

"Volunteerism is something I have carried deeply throughout my life," Tahmina says. "It's what led me to my current work."

Tahmina is a national spokesperson for the American Immigration Lawyers Association (AILA) and the chair of the Response Committee of the Washington Chapter of AILA. Among her honors, she is a recipient of the 2019 AILA President's Commendation Award and an honoree of the 2020 Puget Sound Business Journal Women of Influence.

She is the First Vice President of the Board of King County Bar Association in Washington, a past president of King County Washington Women Lawyers, and a former board member of both the Asian Bar Association of Washington and Washington Women Lawyers. She is also a former member of the Mercer Island School District Superintendent's Diversity Advisory Committee.

Tahmina helped found the Washington Immigration Defense Network, which trains lawyers and facilitates legal representation in the immigration courtroom. She is also co-founder of Airport Lawyer, which was created in response to the first travel ban in January 2017.

Of Bangladeshi heritage, Tahmina brings another valuable skill to her immigration work: her biliteracy in Bengali and fluency in both Hindi and Urdu.

She is the author of *The Startup Visa: Key to Job Growth & Economic Prosperity in America*, and the Amazon bestseller *Legal Heroes in the Era of Trump: Be Inspired, Expand Your Legal Skills, and Leave Your Mark on the World.*

ENDNOTES

PREFACE

1. 51 Million Americans Are Unemployed—Here's The Story Of The Job Seekers Behind The Numbers (forbes.com)
2. Immigrant-Founded Moderna Leading The Way In Covid-19 Response (forbes.com)
3. The Founder Of Pfizer Was An Immigrant, Too (forbes.com)

INTRODUCTION

1. Vivek Wadhwa is a fellow at Rock Center for Corporate Governance at Stanford University, director of research at Center for Entrepreneurship and Research Commercialization at Duke, and distinguished fellow at Singularity University.
2. Vivek Wadhwa, *How Today's Technology is Rapidly Catching Up to Star Trek*, *The Washington Post*, July 1, 2014
3. Tim Kane, *The Importance of Startups in Job Creation and Job Destruction*, Ewing Marion Kauffman Foundation, July 2010.
4. Ibid.
5. Ibid.
6. 2018-BILLION-DOLLAR-STARTUPS.NFAP-Policy-Brief.2018.pdf
7. Dane Stangler and Jared Konczal, *Give Me Your Entrepreneurs, Your Innovators: Estimating the Employment Impact of a Startup Visa*, Ewing
8. Snapdeal Reports Revenue Growth Of 73% In FY2018-19 (inc42.com)
9. American-Made-2.0.pdf (nvca.org)
10. 2018-BILLION-DOLLAR-STARTUPS.NFAP-Policy-Brief.2018.pdf

1. IMMIGRATION AND INNOVATION THROUGH HISTORY

1. https://www.pg.com/en_US/downloads/media/Fact_Sheets_CompanyHistory.pdf
2. Total number of employees of Procter & Gamble worldwide 2007-2020 | Statista
3. http://cprr.org/Museum/Chinese.html
4. http://immigration.about.com/od/successfulimmigrants/p/LeviStrauss.htm
5. Levi Strauss: Number of Employees 2006-2020 | LEVI | MacroTrends

6. Levi Strauss: number of company-operated retail stores, by region worldwide 2019 | Statista
7. Immigration Act of 1917
8. http://www.uscis.gov/tools/glossary/country-limit
9. http://encyclopedia.densho.org/Immigration_Act_of_1952/
10. http://www.forbes.com/companies/bose/
11. Yahoo! - Wikipedia
12. http://www.google.com/about/company/history/https://investor.google.com/corporate/faq.html; https://investor.yahoo.net/faq.cfm;
13. Statistica "Number of full-time Alphabet employees from 2007 to 2020"
14. Macrotrends "EBay: Number of Employees 2006-2020"
15. Macrotrends "PayPal Holdings: Number of Employees 2013-2020"
16. Zoom Revenue and Usage Statistics (2020) - Business of Apps.
17. new-american-fortune-500-june-2011.pdf (newamericaneconomy.org)

2. AROUND THE GLOBE

1. Start-up Visa Program - Canada.ca
2. List of designated organizations – Startup Visa - Canada.ca
3. Shane Phelan, Low take-up in visa scheme to attract wealthy foreigners, Independent. ie, May 26, 2014.
4. Global Impact – Start-Up Chile
5. http://www.independent.ie/irish-news/low-takeup-in-visa-scheme-to-attract-wealthy-foreigners-30304386.html
6. Vivek Wadhwa, Snapdeal- The flourishing company America passed on- offers a lesson about immigration reform, *The Washington Post*, November 7, 2014.
7. Ben Forer and Christine Brouwer, Immigrant Entrepreneur Gets Visa After 'World News' Story, ABC News, November 2, 2011.

3. SQUARE PEGS IN ROUND HOLES

1. In July 2019, the EB-5 rules were amended through regulation and the minimum investments were significantly increased. Federal Register :: EB-5 Immigrant Investor Program Modernization
2. Economic Impact of the EB-5 Regional Center Program (iiusa.org)
3. Canada and Quebec Announce New Investor Programs For Canadian Immigration, Canadian Immigration Newsletter, December 2014.
4. Treaty Country List can be found on the Department of State website: http://travel.state.gov/content/visas/english/fees/treaty.html
5. 8 CFR §214.2(e)(14)
6. Questions & Answers: USCIS Issues Guidance Memorandum on Establishing the "Employee-Employer Relationship" in H-1B Petitions, August 2011. http://www.uscis.gov/news/public-releases-topic/business-immigration/questions-

answersuscis-issues-guidance-memorandum-establishing-employee-employer-rela-
tionship-h-1b-petitions

7. H-1B Visa Denial Rates Remain High But Dropped In 3rd Quarter (forbes.com)
8. USCIS Modifies H-1B Selection Process to Prioritize Wages | USCIS
9. www.watsonimmigrationlaw.com/blog
10. OIG-13-107 Implementation of L-1 Visa Regulations (dhs.gov)
11. DHS Memorandum, Implementation of L-1 Visa Regulations, August 9, 2013.
    http://www.oig.dhs.gov/assets/Mgmt/2013/OIG_13-107_Aug13.pdf
12. http://www.uscis.gov/news/public-releases-topic/business-immigration/
    employment-based-second-preferenceimmigrant-visa-category-frequently-asked-
    questions-regarding-entrepreneurs-and-employment-based-second-preferenceim-
    migrant-visa-category
13. See Matter of New York State Department of Transportation, 22 I&N Dec. 215
    (Comm'r 1998) ("NYSDOT").
14. Matter of DHANASAR, 26 I&N Dec. 884 (AAO 2016) (justice.gov)

4. PITY THE STARTUP FOUNDER

1. USCIS Memorandum, Determining Employer-Employee Relationship for Adjudication of H1b Petitions, Including Third Party Site Placements, Donald
   Neufeld, January 8, 2010. http://www.uscis.gov/sites/default/files/USCIS/
   Laws/Memoranda/2010/H1B%20Employer-Employee%20Memo010810.pdf
2. Visa Bulletin For April 2021 (state.gov)
3. Entrepreneur in Residence, United States Citizenship and Immigration Services
   Initiative Summary, May 2013. http://www.uscis.gov/sites/default/files/
   USCIS/About%20Us/EIR/EntrepreneursinResidence.pdf
4. Treaty Countries (state.gov)
5. Border Security and Immigration Enforcement Improvements- Executive Order
   13767 Federal Register :: Border Security and Immigration Enforcement
   Improvements

5. LEGISLATIVE HISTORY

1. Text - H.R.4259 - 111th Congress (2009-2010): Employment Benefit Act |
   Congress.gov | Library of Congress
2. Polis proposes visa changes in immigration bill – The Denver Post
3. Tahmina Talks Immigration on Apple Podcasts
4. The Founder Visa (paulgraham.com)
5. https://www.congress.gov/bill/113th-congress/house-bill/2131
6. Jennifer Martinez, Issa's tech-backed Skills Visa Act passes House Judiciary panel,
   The Hill, June 28, 2013.
7. Microsoft Word - NFAP Policy Brief.Analysis of Startup Visa Proposals.March 2016

8. To encourage the next Zoom or Moderna, Congress should create a startup visa (washingtonexaminer.com)

6. CHANGES WITHOUT CONGRESS PART I

1. Michael R. Bloomberg, A New Immigration Consensus, Wall Street Journal, May 2, 2011
2. Page 4, final rules.
3. FR_2016-20663_793250_OFR.pdf (uscis.gov)
4. Experienced Seattle Washington Immigration Attorney (watsonimmigrationlaw.com)
5. 2016-20663.pdf (govinfo.gov)
6. Federal Register :: Removal of International Entrepreneur Parole Program
7. Microsoft Word - IER Delay Complaint Final _725148182_26_.DOCX (nvca.org)
8. USCIS to Begin Accepting Applications under the International Entrepreneur Rule | USCIS
9. Tim Kaine, *The Importance of Startups in Job Creation and Job Destruction*, Ewing Marion Kauffman Foundation, July 2010.
10. Jason Wiens, *The Economic Case for Welcoming Entrepreneurs, Kauffman Foundation*, Ewing Marion Kauffman Foundation, September 2015.
11. Research was conducted by Julie Pham, Vice President of Community Engagement & Marketing, Washington Technology Industry Association. Research based on data from Pitchbook on Washington State startups and funding results.
12. https://www.uscis.gov/i-864p
13. S.3029 The Startup Visa Act of 2010
14. http://www.cic.gc.ca/english/immigrate/business/start-up/eligibility.asp
15. http://blakemasters.com/post/21742864570/peter-thiels-cs183-startup-class-6-notes-essay)
16. Ian Harvey, *Companies That Succeeded With Bootstrapping*, Investopedia, August 28, 2014
17. Meghan Casserly, Drybar: *How One Woman and a Hair Dryer became a $20 Million Operation*, Forbes, November 1, 2012.
18. https://www.cbinsights.com/blog/venture-capital-exit-timeframe-tech/
19. http://entrepreneurship.org/resource-center/startup-premoney-valuation--the-keystone-to-return-on-investment.aspx
20. https://www.uscis.gov/working-united-states/known-employer-pilot
21. Much of this text is from the website: https://www.uscis.gov/working-united-states/known-employer-pilot

7. CHANGES WITHOUT CONGRESS PART II

1. Presidential Memorandum -- Modernizing and Streamlining the U.S. Immigrant Visa System for the 21st Century | whitehouse.gov (archives.gov)
2. Federal Register :: Immigration Policy
3. Employment-Based Immigration: Second Preference EB-2 | USCIS
4. Matter of DHANASAR, 26 I&N Dec. 884 (AAO 2016)
5. H.R.8089 - Emergency Stopgap USCIS Stabilization Act (2020)
6. USCIS Memorandum, Interim Guidance for Processing Form I-140 Employ-ment-Based Immigrant Petitions and Form I-485 and H-1B Petitions Affected by the American Competitiveness in the Twenty-First Century Act of 2000 (AC21) (Public Law 106-313), William Yates, May 12, 2005.
7. Visa Bulletin For April 2021 (state.gov)
8. USCIS Memorandum, Determining Employer-Employee Relationship for Adju-dication of H1b Petitions, Including Third Party Site Placements, Donald Neufeld, January 8, 2010.
9. 9 FAM 402.9 TREATY TRADERS, INVESTORS, AND SPECIALTY OCCUPATIONS - E VISAS (state.gov)
10. Immigrant Entrepreneurs: A Path To U.S. Economic Growth, Kauffman Founda-tion, January 22, 2015

CONCLUSION

1. Vivek Wadhwa, With innovators from around the globe digging in, moon travel may be only 20 years away, VentureBeat, January 2, 2015
2. Immigrant Entrepreneurs: A Path to Economic Growth, Kauffman Foundation, January 22, 2015. The report discusses samples of Startup Visas in other countries.
3. Eric Lui made the comment at a live event held at University of Washington School of Law "Race, Immigration and Citizenship," January 14th 2015. He is also the author of The Accidental Asian: Notes of a Native Speaker.

Made in the USA
Monee, IL
20 July 2021